Vocabulary Energizers IV

Stories and Word Origins

David Popkin

VOCABULARY ENERGIZERS IV:
Stories and Word Origins

by David Popkin, Ph. D.

Also by David Popkin:

Vocabulary Energizers
Vocabulary Energizers II
Vocabulary Energizers III

Vocabulary Power Through Shakespeare

Dedication

For my wife Pam
whose wisdom and love transcend words

Vocabulary Energizers IV

ISBN: 978-0-929166-05-6

Second printing: April 2019.

PRINTED IN THE UNITED STATES OF AMERICA

Hada Publications
2605 Belmont Boulevard
Nashville, Tennessee 37212

Contents

Acknowledgements

Thank you Ernest Heard, Myra Ishee, Nancy Rasico, and Jennifer Sohn once again for your critique of the manuscript. I am especially grateful to Mark Ishee for three decades of guidance in bringing my books to fruition.

Preface

"Words, words, words," answers Hamlet to Polonius's question, "Why do you read, my lord?" Welcome to the world of words. Like *Vocabulary Energizers III*, *Vocabulary Energizers IV* is no mere listing of words to be memorized but utilizes words as a gateway to our cultural heritage. Whereas the first two books in the series emphasize the stories behind words, *Vocabulary Energizers III* and *IV* emphasize how words belong to families of Greek and Latin word parts from which they derive. Most importantly, this book remains true to the spirit of its predecessors in that the words are conduits to amusing and informative historical anecdotes. Each of the Units concludes with an essay that reinforces main entry words while introducing world masterpieces from philosophical, religious, and imaginative literature. Thus, *Vocabulary Energizers IV* not only strengthens vocabulary but also welcomes readers to our heritage in the humanities. I hope you enjoy and are enlightened by this book of "words, words, words."

INTRODUCTION
HOW TO USE THIS BOOK

This book has three aims: (1) to increase vocabulary by means of etymological word parts, (2) to acquaint the reader with interesting and significant episodes from history as well as to provide an introduction to classics from literature, philosophy, and the religions of the world, and (3) to promote an interest both in words and our world's cultural achievements.

To achieve these aims, the book is divided into 5 Units, each Unit composed of 2 Lessons, for a total of 10 Lessons in the book. The first Lesson in each Unit lists word parts derived primarily from Greek and Latin (but with the spelling of these word parts as they are most likely to be found in our English words). These word parts, commonly known as roots, convey the main meaning of the word. A page reference for prefixes, which are word parts that come at the beginning of words and precede the roots, appears at the beginning of each lesson for the reader's convenience in deconstructing words. Remember, because of the long history of some English words, the modern meaning of the word might have strayed from its original entry into the language. Therefore, you might have to use your imagination for some words to see how their modern meaning connects with their word parts, although for most words the word parts will be a readily apparent clue to the current meaning of the words.

Main entry words derived from these word parts are then introduced with their definitions and phonetically spelled pronunciations. Where appropriate, the main entry word is followed by "Related Forms," a category which shows the main entry word as it appears in different parts of speech. Following this category is the category "Synonyms," which lists words close in meaning to the main word. The last synonym in the list is phonetically pronounced and can easily be learned by pairing it in the memory with the main entry word. One word of caution: a word rarely has a synonym that is its exact equivalent in meaning. The last synonym listed for each main entry word is a somewhat difficult but useful synonym. I encourage the reader to look up this synonym in a dictionary (preferably one that places the synonym in a context) as well as the others if they want to see the fine shades of difference in meaning. For some main entry words, the category "Antonyms" follows the synonyms. Here again, as with synonyms, a dictionary will help make clear the subtle differences in meaning between antonyms.

Both the main entry word and its phonetically pronounced synonym then appear in the context of a passage that serves as a gateway to political or cultural history. Exercises for the ten main entry words and their ten synonyms conclude the first Lesson of each Unit. The second Lesson for each Unit follows the same pattern as the first, except that the exercises concluding the second lesson for each Unit not only reinforce the words in that Lesson but also review the words in the preceding Lesson as well. The last exercise of each Unit is an essay that, in addition to showing how the words are used, serves as an introduction to either literature, philosophy, or the religions of the world. Thus, the exercises at the end of the second Lesson are a review for the entire Unit. Therefore, Units need to be read as a whole, although the individual Units can be read in any order that is most appealing. Master Exercises following the last Unit of the book provide a comprehensive review for all the words that were previously provided with exercises.

Prefixes

a-, ab-, abs- (not, without; away, from [an- before vowels or h]): abnormal, abstract, anemic, **apathetic, agnostic, abject**

ad-, ac-, etc. (to, toward): admire, access, attract, aggression, **alleviate, assent**

anti- (against, opposite [ant- before vowels or h]): antonym, antiseptic, **antipathy**

con-, com-, co-, etc. (with, together, very): connect, collect, commend, cohabit, **conjecture, consensus**

de- (down, off, away, from): decline, descend, decay, decrease, defend, **dejection**

dis, di-, dif- (apart, in different directions, not): disagree, dispute, different, divorce, **dissent**

en-, em- (in-, into): encourage, energy, employer, emphasize, **empathize**

ex-, e-, ef-, etc. (out, from): exit, eject, efficient expel, **exacerbate**

in-, im-, etc. (not): impossible, immortal, irresponsible, invisible, **irrelevant, incognito**

inter- (between, among): interstate, intercept, interfere, interrupt, **interject**

pre- (before, in front of): predict, prejudice, prevent, **presentiment**

pro- (forward, in front of, for): proceed, proclaim, progress, **prognosticate**

re- (back, again): regain, repeat, reverse, rewrite, remarry, **reprove, reprobate**

se- (aside, away): separate, select, segregate, **seduce**

sub-, suc-, sur-, sus-, etc. (under, beneath): submarine, succumb, suspend, surrogate, **surreptitious**

super- (over, above, beyond): superman, supernatural, supervise, **supersede**

un- (not): unable, unknown, unwelcome, **unremitting**

UNIT 1
LESSON 1

Prefixes in the following words are underlined.
See page xiv for list of prefixes and their definitions.

Word Parts and Words
EU (good, well): euphemism, euphoria, eulogy, euthanasia
TORT (twist): tortuous, distort, retort, extort
SIMIL, SIMUL (like, similar): simulate, facsimile

EU — good, well (the name "Eugene" means "well born")

1. euphemism (YOO fuh miz um) n. pleasant, mild, or inoffensive expression substituted for an unpleasant or offensive one
Related Forms: euphemist, euphemistic, euphemistically
Synonyms: polite term, mild expression, inoffensive substitution, **circumlocution** (sur kum loh KYOO shun)

"Could you tell me where the rest rooms are?" Do we really rest in these rooms? We almost never hear someone ask where do you go to defecate (eliminate solid waste products) or urinate much less the cruder expressions for these terms. Even with children we sometimes use the terms number one and number two or "pee pee" and "pooh pooh" rather than the more technical or vulgar terms. We thus use a **circumlocution** or roundabout way of expressing ourselves to avoid being impolite. Our language has many such **euphemisms** to avoid direct speech that may be offensive.

2. euphoria (yoo FOR ee uh) n. feeling of complete well-being, great happiness, bliss
Related Forms: euphoric, euphorically
Synonyms: happiness, joy, delight, ecstasy, **elation** (ih LAY shun)
Antonyms: misery, depression

The phone rings. Your heart starts beating faster with the expectation that the person you passionately desire has called. Call it infatuation, love, obsession. When we meet this individual, or even think of them, we are filled with intense pleasure or joy. Classic lovers like Romeo and Juliet experience this ecstasy with each other. Popular songs describe the feeling of **elation** when one is in love. Of course, when one gets into the college of their choice or gets offered their ideal job, they, too, experience **euphoria** or **elation**. The Italian poet Dante (1265-1321), in his epic poem *The Divine Comedy* about a man's journey through hell, purgatory, and paradise, depicts the soul's **euphoria** in the heavenly presence of God.

3. eulogy (YOO luh jee) n. speech or writing in praise of someone or something, especially of one who has died
Related Forms: eulogize, eulogizer, eulogist, eulogistic, eulogistically
Synonyms: tribute, praise, accolade, encomium, **panegyric** (pan uh JIR ik)
Antonyms: attack, vilification

Pericles (490-429 B.C.) ruled ancient Athens during the period noted for its contributions to drama, art, philosophy, and science. Under his rule, the Greek city states Athens and Sparta began their conflict with each other—the Peloponnesian War—in 431 B.C., which ended with a Spartan victory in 404 B.C. As recounted by the contemporary Greek historian Thucydides, Pericles gave a great oration at the end of the first year of the war that **eulogized** the dead Athenian soldiers and was also a **panegyric** to the achievements of Athens. Over two millennia later in 1863, President Abraham Lincoln delivered perhaps the most famous of America's wartime **eulogies**, the Gettysburg Address, honoring those who lost their lives in this Civil War battle in Gettysburg, Pennsylvania. The **eulogy** begins, "Four score and seven years ago our fathers brought forth on this continent a new nation" and concludes "that these dead shall not have died in vain, that this nation under God shall have a new birth of freedom, and that government of the people, by the people, and for the people shall not perish from this earth."

4. euthanasia (yoo thuh NAY zhuh) n. mercy killing, painlessly putting to death someone suffering from a prolonged and incurable condition
Related Form: euthanize
Synonyms: assisted suicide, **palliative** (PAL ee uh tiv) dying

Euthanasia is controversial. Physicians assisting in ending life is legal in some countries, illegal in others. When Socrates was sentenced to death and given the poison hemlock to drink, his last words were to his friend Crito, "I owe a cock to Asclepius; will you remember to pay the debt?" One way of interpreting these words may be that Socrates was thankful for a painless death—perhaps a form of **euthanasia** although not one resulting from an incurable and painful disease. Asclepius, son of the Greek god Apollo, was a god of healing. Thus Socrates was telling his friend to honor the god of medicine by offering a sacrificial chicken in gratitude for a **palliative**, pain-free death.

TORT – twist (torment, torture)

5. tortuous (TOR choo us) adj. winding, twisting, full of curves
Related Forms: tortuousness, tortuously
Synonyms: twisty, bending, meandering, serpentine, **sinuous** (SIN yoo us)
Antonyms: straight, direct

In his autobiographical *Old Times on the Mississippi* (1875), Mark Twain recounts his training as a pilot on the Mississippi River. With its many twists and turns often hiding dangerous rocks or tree trunks, this **tortuous** river is difficult to navigate, especially at night. Twain tells the story of two pilots, a Mr. E and his fellow-pilot Mr. X. One evening during a drizzly, dark night Mr. X went off to his bed leaving Mr. E to steer. Approaching a particularly hazardous part of the river, Mr. E, soaked with fear-produced perspiration and rain, was grateful to see Mr. X approach and take over the steering. Calmly and coolly, Mr. X piloted the ship safely through the most precarious parts of the **sinuous** river, silently returned the steering to Mr. E., and went back to bed. Later, Mr. E learned that Mr. X was a somnambulist (sleep walker) and had steered the ship while asleep. Mr. E then exclaimed that if Mr. X "can do such . . . piloting when he is sound asleep, what *couldn't* he do if he were dead."

6. distort (dih STORT) v. twist out of shape; give a false or misleading account or description
Related Forms: distortion, distortive, distortional
Synonyms: twist, deform, misshape, contort, misrepresent, misreport, **misconstrue** (miss kun STROO)

The Bible recounts how Moses sent out twelve spies, one from each of the twelve ancestral tribes of Israel, to see if it were possible for the Israelites to conquer the land of Canaan. Ten of the spies confirmed that this land of milk and honey was indeed rich in crops, but said it would be impossible to conquer since the men of that land were numerous, powerful, and so huge that the spies seemed like grasshoppers in their presence. Two other spies, Caleb and Joshua, then contradict this report as a gross **distortion**. They do not want Moses to **misconstrue** or misinterpret the strength of their enemy. They then argue that the opposing warriors will be easily conquered. Caleb and Joshua's report was accurate and the Israelites eventually invaded and conquered the territory.

7. retort (rih TORT) n., v. sharp, clever, quick reply; reply sharply or cleverly
Synonyms: answer, reply, response, rejoinder, repartee, **riposte** (rih POST)

The Nazi troops of Hitler's Germany ploughed through Europe and conquered or controlled most of the continent's countries during 1939-1941. Not until December 7, 1941, when Japan bombed Pearl Harbor in Hawaii, did the United States enter World War II. During that time England stood almost alone as the sole defender against Hitler's onslaught. England's Prime Minister Winston Churchill manifested bulldog determination as he roused his nation to defend itself. Known for his stirring oratory and masterly writing—in 1953 receiving the Nobel Prize for literature—Churchill was the face of defiant opposition to Hitler. But he was also famous for his sharp humor and biting repartees or **retorts**. Once when told by a female social acquaintance that if he were her husband she would poison his coffee, Churchill replied with the **riposte** that if she were his wife he would drink that coffee.

8. extort (ik STORT) v. get by force or threat
Related Forms: extortion, extortionist, extorter
Synonyms: force, extract, squeeze, wring, wrest, **coerce** (koh URS)

Fear of witches propels American playwright Arthur Miller's *The Crucible* (1953), a drama based on a famous witch trial in Salem,

Massachusetts, in the seventeenth century. At one point, Giles Corey, a farmer in his eighties, is **coerced** into answering a charge whether or not he is a witch. He refuses to answer so as to insure that his children will inherit his land. The authorities torture him by pressing heavy weights on his chest to **extort** either a confession or denial, but Corey remains silent. Finally, as they continue to press for a response, he answers, “More weight,” and dies.

SIMIL, SIMUL — like, similar (similar, simultaneous)

9. simulate (SIM yuh layt) v. create the affect, appearance, feeling or behavior of
Related Forms: simulation, simulator, simulative
Synonyms: imitate, reproduce, duplicate, mimic, replicate, fake, pretend, **feign** (FAYN)

According to an ancient Greek myth, Zeus (king of the gods) and Hermes (messenger of the gods) decided to descend to earth and **simulate** the appearance of mere mortals to see if they would receive hospitality in a certain region. Everyone closed their homes to them except an old man named Baucis and his elderly wife Philemon. They provided the two gods, **feigning** to be desolate wanderers, with as sumptuous a feast as their poor home could offer. They even amused the two Olympians as the old couple unsuccessfully scrambled to capture a goose for the meal. At last the gods no longer **simulated** or **feigned** human identity and revealed their true selves. They drowned the rest of the inhabitants of the area by turning the valley into a lake and rewarded the old couple by granting them a wish. The couple asked to be priests in a temple devoted to these gods and to be allowed to die together. Their wish was granted, and when they died, they were transformed into a linden and oak tree that grew from a single trunk so that they could remain with each other.

10. facsimile (fak SIM uh lee) n. exact copy or something closely resembling something else
Synonyms: copy, reproduction, duplicate, **replica** (REP lih kuh)
Antonym: original

If you were to find an exact copy of the Declaration of Independence on old parchment you might feel that you had a priceless treasure. Similarly, someone may show you what looks like an original copy of the Gettysburg Address. However, these **facsimiles** are often sold as souvenir items. Sometimes, if the **facsimile** itself is very old, it may take an expert to determine whether it is an original. Whereas the word "**facsimile**" is usually associated with printed material like letters and books, exact copies of objects such as sculpture and furniture are commonly referred to as **replicas**. Do not be fooled into spending a fortune on a **facsimile** of a first edition of Chaucer's *The Canterbury Tales* or a **replica** of the Italian Renaissance artist Michelangelo's sculpture *David.*

WORKING WITH WORDS

UNIT 1, LESSON 1

I. Complete the sentences by using each of the following words once:
tortuous, facsimile, euphemism, extort, retort, euphoria, euthanasia, eulogy, simulate, distort

1. Why do we reserve our praise for those dear to us in a ____________ after their death rather than tell them how much they mean to us while they are alive?

2. The straight roads of the highways contrast with the ____________ roads winding about the mountain.

3. The officials managed to ____________ a confession by torturing their subject.

4. The ____________ of the ancient document was so good that I could not distinguish it from the original.

5. Do people really rest in a "rest room," or is it a ____________ for something else?

6. We feared asking our professor a question for he often gave us a sharp ____________ .

7. Would you prefer ____________ or suffering a long and painful death from an incurable disease?

8. I learned to pilot a plane by first practicing on a computer that would ____________ flight.

9. When taking a bath and finding that the volume of his body displaced an equal volume of water, the ancient Greek mathematician and scientist Archimedes experienced ____________ at his discovery, stepped out of the bath, and ran naked through the streets joyously exclaiming "Eureka!" (I have found it).

10. My opponents ____________ what I say so that many people have a false view of my ideas.

II. This exercise reinforces the difficult synonyms in boldface accompanying the main words derived from word parts. Select the two words that are synonyms.

1. a. twisting b. sinuous
   c. warm d. happy

2. a. transportation b. destruction
   c. circumlocution d. roundabout way of expression

3. a. riposte b. wound
   c. question d. quick and clever reply

4. a. attack b. praise
   c. panegyric d. blame

5. a. copy b. discovery
   c. consciousness d. replica

6. a. palliative dying b. burial
   c. assisted suicide d. funeral speech

7. a. sickness b. elation
   c. sadness d. joy

8. a. obey b. feign
   c. disagree d. fake

9. a. misconstrue b. trust
   c. threaten d. misinterpret

10. a. assist b. coerce
    c. force d. educate

UNIT 1
LESSON 2

Prefixes in the following words are underlined.
See page xiv for list of prefixes and their definitions.

Word Parts and Words
SIMIL, SIMUL (like, similar): assimilate, simile
PORT (carry): importune, rapport, portly, portend
TOM (cut): epitome, dichotomy, tome, entomology

SIMI, SIMUL — like, similar (similar, simultaneous)

11. assimilate (uh SIM uh layt) v. absorb; take in; learn thoroughly
Related Forms: assimilation, assimilator
Synonyms: merge, blend in, incorporate, integrate, comprehend, **homogenize** (hoh MOJ uh nyz)
Antonyms: reject, isolate, separate, segregate

In her autobiographical writings, the Native American Zitkala-Sa (1876-1938), also known as Gertrude Bonnin, recounts how she was taken away from her traditional upbringing at the age of eight and taken to a missionary school. Here she was shorn of her braids, had her moccasins exchanged for shoes, learned English, and was taught a religion new to her. With the loss of her braids on the first day at school, Zitkala-Sa also lost her spirit since only mourners, unskilled warriors captured by enemies, and cowards were associated with lost hair in her Indian tradition. This event was an extreme case of **assimilation** into the dominant American culture. When different ethnic groups come to a new country, there is always the question of how they will be **assimilated**. Do we want newcomers to shed their identities and blend into a common, **homogenous** melting pot, or do we want them to retain their identities and become more like distinct items in a tasty stew?

12. simile (SIM uh lee) n. comparison of one thing with another using "like" or "as"
Synonyms: comparison, parallel, **analogy** (uh NAL uh jee)

Charles Dickens's famous tale *A Christmas Carol* tells us at its beginning,

> Old Marley [Scrooge's former business partner] was dead as a door-nail. Mind! I don't mean to say that I know, of my own knowledge, what there is particularly dead about a door-nail. I might have been inclined, myself, to regard a coffin-nail as the deadest piece of ironmongery in the trade. But the wisdom of our ancestors is in the **simile** . . . .

If Dickens had written "Old Marley was a dead door-nail," he would have changed the original simile ("dead as a door-nail") to a metaphor. Shakespeare's comic drama *As You Like It*, has these often quoted lines,

> All the world's a stage,
> And all the men and women merely players [actors],
> They have their exits and their entrances,
> And one man in his time plays many parts . . . .

If the metaphor "all the world's a stage, and all the men and women merely players" had been changed to "all the world is like a stage, and all the men and women merely like players," then the original metaphor would have been changed to a **simile**. Thus, the little words "like" and "as" determine whether an **analogy** or comparison is a **simile** or metaphor.

PORT — carry (export, import, report, support)

13. importune (im pur TOON) v. beg, urge, request repeatedly, sometimes in an annoying way

Related Forms: importuner, importunateness, importunate, importunately

Synonyms: beg, request, ask, plead, beseech, implore, supplicate, **entreat** (en TREET)

The Bible tells how Abraham's wife Sarah continually **importuned** Abraham to send away her maid servant Hagar and her son Ishmael. Sarah had given Abraham permission to have a child with Hagar when previously Sarah had thought she was barren. However, Sarah went on to give birth to Isaac when she was ninety years old. She then begged, pleaded, pestered, implored, and **entreated** Abraham until he finally cast off Hagar and Ishmael to the desert. Similarly, the Bible describes how Samson was repeatedly implored and **importuned** by Delilah until he revealed that the secret of his strength was in his hair, which she then had cut off when Samson slept. A story from Greek mythology shows how Phaethon went to the sun-god Helius to confirm that he was indeed his son. Helius said yes and he would grant Phaethon anything he desired. The boy then asked Helius to be allowed to drive the chariot with the sun across the sky. Helius repeatedly implored and **entreated** his son to wish for something else. Phaethon refused no matter how much his father **importuned**. Phaethon then drove the chariot across the sky, lost control of the horses, and was blasted by Zeus's thunderbolt to prevent the chariot from incinerating the earth.

14. rapport (rah POR) n. harmonious or sympathetic relationship
Synonyms: understanding, relationship, bond,
camaraderie (kah muh RAH duh ree)
Antonyms: hostility, incompatibility, antagonism

One of the world's oldest myths is the Mesopotamian epic *Gilgamesh.* Gilgamesh, the hero of this story, begins as a cruel, tyrannical king. To humble him, the gods create a wild man, Enkidu, to wrestle Gilgamesh. After a prolonged, nearly even struggle, the two are filled with respect and admiration for each other. They develop a close **rapport** and go adventuring together. The **camaraderie** lasts until Enkidu's death. The loss of his best friend throws Gilgamesh into intense anguish that he too will die. Gilgamesh then goes on an unsuccessful quest to discover immortality. The **rapport** of Gilgamesh and Enkidu reminds us of other famous literary **comradeships**, such as those of Sherlock Holmes and Dr. Watson, Huckleberry Finn and Jim, and Don Quixote and Sancho Panza.

15. portly (PORT lee) n. somewhat heavy, or fat
Related Form: portliness
Synonyms: plump, chubby, stout, fat, rotund, **obese** (oh BEES)
Antonyms: slim, thin, lean, slender, skinny

England's Prime Minister Winston Churchill was a bit **portly** in appearance. Even more **portly** is the conventional image of Santa Claus. However, **portly** conveys the idea of a somewhat rounded figure or substantial stomach girth, not of being grossly overweight or excessively fat, a condition described as **obese**. William Howard Taft, the heaviest U. S. president (1909-1913) at about six feet tall weighed over three hundred pounds. There are stories that his great bulk caused him to get stuck in a White House bath tub as well as in a bath tub that he used while visiting the Belle Meade Mansion in Nashville, Tennessee. Perhaps Taft could be kindly described as **portly**, but **obese** would not be inappropriate. This rotund individual later became the only former president to be appointed chief justice of the Supreme Court.

16. portend (por TEND) v. be a sign, warning, or omen of
Related Forms: portent, portentous, portentously
Synonyms: foreshadow, foretell, forecast, predict, **presage** (PRES ij)

Oedipus Rex (*Oedipus the King*) by Sophocles is perhaps the most well-known play of ancient Greece. Before having any children, Oedipus's father, Laius, went to an oracle. The oracle interpreted signs that **portended** that Laius would be killed by his own son. When Oedipus was born, King Laius, recalling what the oracle had **presaged**, ordered the infant to be taken to the forest and left to die. However, a shepherd came upon the infant and took him to another country where he was raised by a king and queen who never told Oedipus that he was adopted. Later, as a young man, Oedipus went to an oracle who revealed **portents** that Oedipus would kill his father and marry his mother. Horrified, Oedipus fled the country where he was raised and came to the country where his biological parents ruled. Through an ironic unfolding of events, the tragic outcome **presaged** to Laius was fulfilled.

TOM — cut (anatomy, atom, appendectomy, hysterectomy)

17. epitome (ih PIT uh mee) n. perfect example
Related Form: epitomize
Synonyms: model, example, exemplar, paragon,
embodiment (em BOD ee ment)

The biblical Samson and the Greek mythological hero Hercules are **epitomes** of the strong man. Both killed lions with their bare hands. Just as they are **embodiments** of physical strength, so is Helen of Troy—for whom the Trojan War was fought between the Greeks and the Trojans in Homer's *Iliad*—the **epitome** of female physical beauty. Christopher Marlowe, English playwright and contemporary of Shakespeare, pays tribute to her in his play *Dr. Faustus*, about a learned man Faustus who sells his soul to the devil. In this play, the devil conjures up the image of Helen. Faustus greets this **epitome** or **embodiment** of beauty with these words, "Was this the face that launched a thousand ships . . . ."

18. dichotomy (dy KOT uh mee) n. division into two parts, often contradictory and mutually exclusive
Related Form: dichotomous
Synonyms: division, split, difference, contrast, chasm,
schism (SKIZ um)

"Is he a good guy?" Children often ask this question. They want a simple **dichotomy** between who is good and who is bad. Adults, too, are prone to this tendency as illustrated by the good angel with a halo on one shoulder and the bad angel or horned devil on the other trying to persuade someone to make a moral or immoral choice. Christopher Marlowe's character Faustus has a good angel and an evil angel wrestling for his soul before he succumbs to the persuasion of the evil angel and signs his compact with Mephistopheles, servant to Lucifer (Satan). Political candidates often portray great **schisms** between themselves and their opponents, sometimes even demonizing the opposition. Reality, however, is usually more complex than the simple **dichotomy** of black versus white.

19. tome (TOHM) n. large, heavy book or volume
Synonyms: volume, book, **opus** (OH pus)

20. entomology (en tuh MOL uh jee) n. study of insects
Related Forms: entomologist, entomological, entomologically
NOT a synonym: **etymology** (et uh MAL uh jee - do not confuse "entomology" with "etymology," the study of word origins or the derivation of words)

The word part *tom* meaning "cut" can be found in many operations, such as appendectomy for removing the appendix and tonsillectomy for removing the tonsils. From the slicing or cutting roles of paper to make pages, we get the word "**tome**" for a massive book. F. Scott Fitzgerald's novel *The Great Gatsby* (1925) portrays the excesses of America's "Jazz Age." In one scene the narrator Nick Carraway enters the library in the mansion of Jay Gatsby (the novel's main character who has attained fabulous wealth through the illegal selling of alcohol). The room is filled with shelf upon shelf of books. Nick discovers all the books, whether slim volumes or fat **tomes**, have never been read. In those days, new books sometimes came with uncut pages which were separated by cutting with a knife as one read. Thus Gatsby's library is merely a magnificent show, no one having made practical use of it. We also see the use of the word part *tom* in the **etymology** or word origin of **entomology** (*en* = in, *tom* = cut, *logy* = study of). **Entomology** is the scientific study of insects, life forms that seem to be cut into segments (some insects have clear divisions between their heads and abdomens). Interestingly, the **etymology** of the word "insect" is from the word parts *in* = in and *sect* = cut. Whereas the **etymology** of **entomology** comes from Greek word parts, the **etymology** of insect comes from Latin. A famous **entomologist** E. O. Wilson from Harvard wrote a massive book or **tome** on ants, perhaps regarded by some as his **opus** or major work, although he has also written books that make major contributions to evolutionary theory. Remember, that although the word "**opus**" can refer to a writer's major work, it is more often used to refer to the work of a musical composer.

WORKING WITH WORDS

UNIT 1, LESSONS 1 & 2

The following exercises include all main words derived from word parts and their synonyms in boldface from both Lessons 1 and 2.

1. Match the word on the left with its synonym.

Set 1

_i_ 1. euphoria	a. presage, foretell
_b_ 2. extort	b. twisting, sinuous
_f_ 3. simulate	c. analogy, comparison
_g_ 4. dichotomy	d. panegyric, tribute
_c_ 5. simile	e. misconstrue, misrepresent
_h_ 6. tortuous	f. entreat, implore
_d_ 7. eulogy	g. schism, division
_j_ 8. importune	h. coerce, force
_e_ 9. distort	i. elation, ecstasy
_a_ 10. portend	j. feign, imitate

Set 2

_a_ 1. euphemism	a. riposte, reply
_e_ 2. facsimile	b. camaraderie, relationship
_h_ 3. epitome	c. homogenize, integrate
_j_ 4. retort	d. palliative dying, assisted suicide
_i_ 5. portly	e. replica, copy
_c_ 6. assimilate	f. opus, book
_b_ 7. rapport	g. insect science, bug study
_g_ 8. entomology	h. embodiment, model
_f_ 9. tome	i. obese, fat
_d_ 10. euthanasia	j. circumlocution, inoffensive substitution

II. Complete the sentences by using each of the following words once:

Set 1 Words:
euthanasia, assimilating, euphoria, dichotomy, portly, entomologist, distorted, retorted, importuned, simulates

1. When the woman I loved said "yes" to my marriage proposal, I felt _____euphoria_____ .

2. Why is Katherine so interested in bugs? Is she going to be an _____entomologist_____ ?

3. No matter how much I _____assimilate_____ my parents to get me a car for my graduation, they refused to grant my wish.

4. Can you tell the difference between when someone sincerely says he loves you and when he _____simulates_____ ?

5. How do you feel about your country _____portly_____ a large number of immigrants whose ethnicity is so different from your own?

6. When I asked my biology teacher why I could not find the muscles on the fetal pig I dissected, she sarcastically _____retorted_____ that I should look in the garbage pail where I had thrown the skin I had cut off.

7. Do you think _____euthanasia_____ is justified when someone is suffering from an excruciatingly painful and incurable disease?

8. Propaganda causes us to have a _____distorted_____ view of reality.

9. There is a sharp _____dichotomy_____ between the political views of my father and my uncle which often leads to fierce arguments when they get together.

10. The doctor advised my _____importuned_____ son-in-law to go on a diet in order to lower his blood pressure.

Set 2 Words:
euphemism, rapport, simile, portend, extort, tortuous, facsimile, epitome, tome, eulogy

1. I enjoy walking along ______________ trails more than on straight city streets.

2. "My grandmother passed away" is a ______________ for "my grandmother died."

3. Better to let people that you like know how much you appreciate them while they are alive than to wait until they are dead to praise them in a ______________ .

4. Do you think it is important for teachers to have a good ______________ with their students?

5. My expectations for making a fortune were shattered when I learned that the treaty I found of the 1803 Louisiana Purchase was not the original but a ______________ .

6. "My boss is like a raging bull" is a ______________ ; "my boss is a raging bull" is a metaphor.

7. Albert Einstein is the ______________ of a scientific genius.

8. The darkening clouds and gusty winds ______________ that today would be a disaster to have a picnic.

9. The ancient ______________ could not be read in a day but would take weeks of study to plough through and assimilate.

10. Using torture and threats to kill the man's family, corrupt officials tried to ______________ a confession from their innocent victim.

III. *THE MERCHANT OF VENICE* AND *THE BLUEST EYE*: RELIGIOUS AND RACIAL DIVISION
Fill in each blank by using each of the following only once:

Set 1 Words:
facsimile, rapport, portends, extortion, assimilation, simulates, entomologist, dichotomy, distorts, tomes

Can a society of diverse ethnic, racial, and religious groups function justly and harmoniously, preserving the dignity and uniqueness of each group? Minorities have often suffered as the majority tends to oppress and even instill a negative self-image in minority individuals. The problem of__________ or the absorption of a minority within a larger group, whether religious or racial, is depicted in Shakespeare's play *The Merchant of Venice* and the first novel of America's Nobel Prize-winning novelist Toni Morrison, *The Bluest Eye* (1970). As Martin Luther King, Jr., pointed out, discrimination __________ or misrepresents reality, giving a false sense of superiority to the majority and a false sense of inferiority to the minority. Why is this so? The __________ or insect-studying scientist Edwin O. Wilson is one of several researchers who have theorized that cooperation within a group was an evolutionary advantage to that group's survival. Evolution thus favored altruistic or benevolent behavior of individuals to each other within the group. However, this kindly behavior did not extend to other groups, since groups were in competition with each other for survival. Thus we have the __________ or contrast between our charitable, selfless behavior with that of our aggressive and ruthless actions. The former is often extended to those within our group, the later frequently manifested toward outsiders. *The Merchant of Venice* and *The Bluest Eye* illustrate these social dynamics.

In Shakespeare's play, the rich merchant Antonio and his younger friend Bassanio have an excellent __________ or close relationship with one another. Bassanio confides in Antonio that he is wooing a young, beautiful, and fabulously wealthy heiress named Portia.

However, Bassanio, somewhat of a spendthrift, has exhausted his fortune and needs more money to continue his wooing. Antonio unhesitatingly agrees to give him the money, but there is a problem. Right now Antonio has invested all his funds in ships at sea for commercial ventures. He expects to make huge profits when the ships return. Therefore, he tells Bassanio to use his name in order to get funds from a moneylender. An arrangement is made by which the Jewish moneylender Shylock will give three thousand ducats (a sum that could buy a house) if Antonio will sign a bond saying that he will repay the loan within three months at no interest. Sounds generous, but wait. Shylock has long harbored a hatred for the merchant. The Christian Antonio has spit upon and kicked Shylock in the past, as well as thwarted some of his business deals. Why? All for the reason that Shylock is Jewish. Since the Middle Ages, Christianity had regarded lending money at interest as a sin. However, Jews did not share this viewpoint. Therefore, for many years Jews had almost a monopoly on usury, or the lending of money at interest. Since at this time Jews were not allowed to own land in Christian communities or to enter the Christian guilds that would train them in a professional craft, money lending was one of the few means available to them to earn a living. Along with the usual fear and distrust one has for strangers—xenophobia (fear or hatred of strangers and foreigners, from *xen* = stranger, foreigner + *phob* = fear)—negative feelings were amplified toward Jews because of their association with interest loans. Now is Shylock's chance to get even with the man who has despised and demeaned him. He offers a three month loan with no interest if Antonio will agree to one condition. If the loan is not paid back on time, Shylock can take a pound of flesh from anywhere on Antonio's body. Bassanio realizes that such an agreement __________ or foreshadows some disaster and urges his friend not to sign the contract. Antonio, confident that he will make at least three times the sum when his ships return, signs the bond.

Soon afterward, Shylock's daughter Jessica, possessed with the negative self-image that Christian society has instilled in her of being a Jew, renounces her faith, steals her father's money and jewelry, and runs away with a Christian lover to become a Christian wife. In order to do so, she ______________ or fakes the appearance of a boy by dressing in male clothing so that she can elope undetected. Heartbroken, Shylock is now set on vengeance if Antonio forfeits his loan.

When it becomes apparent that Antonio cannot fulfill the contract because he has lost a ship and others have not yet returned, two of Antonio's friends tell Shylock that he will surely not demand Antonio's flesh for what good would that do? To which Shylock answers,

> To bait fish withal: if it will feed nothing else, it will feed my revenge. He [Antonio] hath disgraced me, and hindered me half a million, laughed at my losses, mocked at my gains, scorned my nation, thwarted my bargains, cooled my friends, heated mine enemies; and what's his reason? I am a Jew. Hath not a Jew hands, organs, dimensions, senses, affections, passions? Fed with the same food, hurt with the same weapons, subject to the same diseases, healed by the same means, warmed and cooled by the same winter and summer, as a Christian is? If you prick us do we not bleed? If you tickle us do we not laugh? If you poison us do we not die? And if you wrong us, shall we not revenge? If we are like you in the rest, we will resemble you in that. If a Jew wrong a Christian, what is his humility [i.e., what does a Christian do, does he bear his suffering with humility]? Revenge! If a Christian wrong a Jew, what should his sufferance be by Christian example? Why, revenge! The villainy you teach me I will execute, and it shall go hard but I will better the instruction.

Shylock's tirade is that of any oppressed person against his oppressors. Despite attempts of those in power to dehumanize those who differ–whether it be in class, religion, race, or nationality—the speech asserts the full humanity of the disadvantaged. Ironically, Shylock has learned only one thing from a Christianity that preaches charity and forgiveness—revenge.

Antonio then stands trial for failure to pay back his loan. Defending Antonio is Portia, now Bassanio's wife, but disguised as and simulating a male lawyer because only men were lawyers at that time. Presumably, she has a reputation as very learned, having mastered the __________ or books of law. She importunes Shylock to take three times the money owed to him offered by Bassanio who now has become wealthy because of marriage. However, Shylock examines the original bond—not a __________ or copy—finds that he is entitled to his pound of flesh and does not even have to stop the bleeding. As he whets his knife and prepares to pierce Antonio's heart, Portia stops him. She points out that the contract says that Shylock is entitled to a pound of flesh but not to even a jot of blood. If he does cause bleeding, he will be accused of killing a citizen of Venice and will therefore himself be executed as a murderer. Through this means of __________ or threat on Shylock's life, Antonio is freed, Shylock forced to forfeit a large sum of his fortune and to convert to Christianity.

Set 2 Words:
tortuous, epitome, euthanasia, retort, simile, euphoric, portly, eulogy, euphemism, importunes

Whereas *The Merchant of Venice* focuses on the situation of Jews in Christian society during the Renaissance and portrays the disdain Shylock's daughter Jessica has for her own Jewishness, *The Bluest Eye* portrays the self-hatred and contempt for their skin color that some African Americans felt in the 1930s and 1940s because of the racial atmosphere in America. The blue eyes, blond hair, and Caucasian features compose the __________ or perfect example of feminine beauty. The novel focuses on Pecola Breedlove, about eleven or twelve, who is scorned even by her own community for her dark complexion and deviation from the standards of white beauty. To others in her neighborhood she epitomizes ugliness. Her strongest desire is to have blue eyes, whose possession would make her ________________ or ecstatic.

Sharply contrasting with Pecola is Maureen Peal, an African American schoolmate who is relatively light skinned and whose features conform to the ideal of white beauty that has been internalized by some African Americans who denigrate or belittle themselves. Claudia MacTeer, the nine-year-old narrator of the story, dislikes the haughty Maureen. When Maureen insults Claudia, her sister Frieda, and Pecola by calling them "black and ugly," Maureen and Frieda ________________ or sharply reply by twisting Maureen Peal's name into "Meringue Pie."

The only adults who show some affection for Pecola are "three ladies of the evening," a ________________ or polite expression for "prostitutes, whores." One of these women, Marie, can be politely described as ________________, or less politely as grossly fat. When Pecola comes without socks to Marie, the obese Marie greets her with the striking ________________ or comparison, "You as barelegged as a yard dog."

In part, the negative self-image of the hunched, downcast Pecola has been reinforced by her abusive father, Cholly Breedlove. Cholly himself has lived a ________________ or twisted existence in which life has thrown him many curves. Abandoned by his parents as an infant, Cholly was raised by a great aunt. At fourteen, during his first experience of sexual intercourse with a young girl, two white men come upon them. They throw their flashlight on the couple and mockingly force Cholly at gunpoint to continue the sexual act. The traumatized Cholly can only simulate or feign intercourse.

Years later, in a drunken stupor, Cholly rapes his daughter Pecola and makes her pregnant. Looking for solace, Pecola comes to Soaphead Church, a phony spiritualist and psychic reader. Soaphead hates his landlord's old dog and convinces himself that it would be a humane act to poison the dog, thus performing a benevolent ________________ or mercy killing. Soaphead uses Pecola as the vehicle for this act. When she ________________ or begs him to give her blue eyes, he gives her poisoned food to feed to the dog and tells her if the dog then behaves strangely her wish will be granted. The poisoned dog undergoes a violent spasm and dies. Convinced, Pecola believes her eyes will become blue. Eventually she goes insane, certain that her eyes are blue, and gives birth to a premature baby who dies. Like the dog whom Pecola unintentionally killed, her baby receives no ____________ or funeral praise. Shakespeare and Toni Morrison both show the tragic consequences of a society whose powerful majority oppresses a minority and inflicts upon them a destructive self-image.

UNIT 2
LESSON 3

Prefixes in the following words are underlined.
See page xiv for list of prefixes and their definitions.

Word Parts and Words
ARCH (ruler, govern): anarchy, hierarchy, monarch, matriarch
FID (faith, trust): fidelity, perfidy, diffident, bona fide
HER, HES (stick, cling): coherent, incoherent

ARCH — ruler, govern (architect, archbishop)

1. **anarchy** (AN ur kee) n. absence of government or law; confusion, disorder
Related Forms: anarchism, anarchist, anarchistic, anarchic, anarchical, anarchically
Synonyms: lawlessness, disorder, chaos, **nihilism** (NY uh liz um)
Antonyms: government, order

Things fall apart; the centre cannot hold;
Mere **anarchy** is loosed upon the world.

These lines from "The Second Coming" by the Irish poet William Butler Yeats (1865-1939) describe the collapse of civilization approximately two thousand years after the birth of Jesus. The poem foretells how after "twenty centuries of stony sleep" there will be a Second Coming as a

...rough beast, its hour come round at last,
Slouches toward Bethlehem to be born.

Chaos, destruction, and **anarchy** await us. The rejection of religious and moral principles, as well as the collapse of political and social institutions creates an atmosphere of **nihilism** or the absence of belief in traditional values and practices. The threat of **anarchy** or **nihilism** is portrayed in many twentieth-century writers. Joseph Conrad, a Polish immigrant to England and masterful stylist of the English language, depicts the ruthless exploitation of Africa by European imperialists in his novel *Heart of Darkness*. The Nigerian Chinua Achebe's novel *Things Fall Apart* (the title echoing Yeats's poem) portrays the **anarchy** and **nihilism** that is loosed upon a traditional Nigerian village as its structures and values fall under the pressure of Western incursion.

2. hierarchy (HY uh rar kee) n. person or things arranged in a graded series or rank

Related Forms: hierarchal, hierarchic, hierarchical, hierarchically

Synonyms: ranking, gradation, scale, **pecking** (PEK ing) **order**

Biologists have observed **hierarchies** in several species. There is an order of rank in wolves and chimpanzees. We know that there are alpha males and alpha females in wolf packs that lead the group. Hens peck on other hens that are inferior to them in rank while submitting to the pecking of hens that rank above them. From this activity we get the term "**pecking order**" that refers to a ranked series or **hierarchy**. Irish-born British playwright George Bernard Shaw (1856-1950), best known for his play *Pygmalion* which was made into the musical *My Fair Lady*, wrote *Major Barbara* that superbly describes **hierarchies** or **pecking orders**. This play is about a woman who works for the Salvation Army and whose father, Andrew Undershaft, is one of the world's richest men because he manufactures weapons for various nations. In answer to a question about how he keeps discipline among his workers, Undershaft answers,

> I don't. They do. You see, the one thing [a man] won't stand is any rebellion from the man under him . . . . Of course they all rebel against me, theoretically. Practically, every man of them keeps the man just below him in place . . . . The men

> snub the boys and order them about; the carmen snub the sweepers; the artisans snub the unskilled laborers; the foremen drive and bully both the laborers and the artisans; the assistant engineers find fault with the foremen; the chief engineers drop on the assistants; the department managers worry the chiefs . . . . The result is a colossal profit which comes to me.

3. monarch (MON urk) n. ruler or person who holds a dominant position, especially a hereditary ruler like a king, queen, emperor or sultan

Related Forms: monarchy, monarchism, monarchal, monarchic, monarchical, monarchically

Synonyms: ruler, sovereign, **potentate** (POHT un tayt)

Some of history's most famous **monarchs** are Alexander the Great, Peter the Great of Russia, Queen Elizabeth I of England, Napoleon of France, and the Mongol ruler Kublai Khan (1216-1294). This last **potentate** completed his grandfather Genghis Kahn's conquest of China and conquered much of southeastern Asia. The Italian Marco Polo left his country at the age of seventeen and returned over twenty years later, having spent the majority of that time in Kublai Khan's empire. After returning to Italy, Marco Polo wrote about his travels and the **potentate's** court. Polo described such things in China as paper money and the mining of coal for fuel that were unknown to his European contemporaries. The **monarchs** of the West had much to learn from the **potentate** Kublai Khan. The English poet Samuel Taylor Coleridge, famous for "The Rime of the Ancient Mariner," paid tribute to the Mongol **monarch** in the poem "Kubla Khan," which begins,

> In Xanadu did Kubla Kahn
> A stately pleasure dome decree:
> Where Alph, the sacred river, ran
> Through caverns measureless to man
> Down to a sunless sea.

4. matriarch (MAY tree ark) n. woman who rules a family, clan, tribe, or group
Related Forms: matriarchy, matriarchal, matriarchic
Synonyms: female in charge, female leader, **matron** (MAY trun)

Patriarchs are male rulers. Abraham, Isaac, and Jacob are Jewish patriarchs in the Bible. **Matriarchs** are the female counterparts of patriarchs. Anthropologists tell us that some cultures were ruled by patriarchs, some by **matriarchs**. The twentieth-century play *A Raisin in the Sun* by the African American Lorraine Hansberry describes a family of a man, his wife, their young son and the man's sister living together in the apartment of the man and his sister's mother, the **matriarch** of the family. As they endure the trials of poverty, the possibility of abortion, and resistance to moving into a white community, it is the **matron**, the grandmother Lena Younger, who holds the family together. At one point when her intellectual, idealistic, college-educated daughter who hopes to be a doctor declares that humans alone have improved their condition without the aid of a supernatural power, the **matriarch**, a traditional believer, asserts her authority by slapping her daughter in the face and forcing her to repeat, “In my mother's house there is still a God.” This **matron** may be at odds with the views of the younger generation, but she proves a wise **matriarch** who enables her family to be the best they can be.

FID — faith, trust (confidence, confident)

5. fidelity (fih DEL ih tee) n. faithfulness, loyalty
Synonyms: devotion, allegiance, **steadfastness** (STED fast ness)
Antonyms: faithlessness, infidelity, disloyalty

6. perfidy (PUR fih dee) n. treachery, betrayal
Related Forms: perfidious, perfidiously
Synonyms: faithlessness, treason, disloyalty, deceit, **duplicity** (doo PLISS uh tee)

From the word part *fid* meaning "faith" we get the name "Fido," a common name for a dog since it expresses the **fidelity** and devotion we associate with "man's best friend." In the Bible, King David sees the beautiful Bathsheba, wife of David's soldier Uriah. While Uriah is away fighting, David lusts for Bathsheba and gets her pregnant—clearly a **perfidious** act toward his soldier. Attempting to cover up the adultery, David invites Uriah back from the war, feasts him, and even gets him drunk. He then tells Uriah to go home to his wife so that by sleeping with her Uriah will be assumed to have made her pregnant. However, Uriah is extremely loyal and **steadfast** to his commander and fellow soldiers. He refuses to go home to his wife while his comrades are risking their lives on the battlefield. He considers such an action **perfidy** or treachery to his fellow warriors. Unable to get Uriah to cooperate in his **duplicitous** scheme, David sends Uriah back to war, orders Uriah's general to send the soldier to the front lines and then withdraw support so as to ensure Uriah's death. This plan succeeds. Later King David is denounced by the prophet Nathan for his infidelity or adultery with Bathsheba and his **perfidious** commands leading to Uriah's death. King David could easily have had Nathan killed, but he repents his infidelity and **perfidy**, fasts, prays, and atones for his sin.

7. diffident (DIF uh dent) adj. lacking self-confidence; timid; unassertive
Related Forms: diffidence, diffidently
Synonyms: shy, insecure, **timorous** (TIM uh rus)
Antonyms: confident, assured, bold

If you have confidence you have faith in yourself and feel secure; if you are **diffident** you are lacking faith and shy or insecure. One of America's preeminent historians, John Hope Franklin (1915-2009), especially noted for his classic study of African American history *From Slavery to Freedom*, told this story to an audience at Fisk University (his alma mater) of his first encounter with W. E. B. DuBois (1868-1963), a pioneer in African American history, sociology, and the civil rights movement. Franklin was a young graduate student at the time and DuBois was his hero. DuBois was the spokesperson for many African American intellectuals who demanded full political, social, and educational rights immediately rather than following the more conciliatory position of Booker T. Washington's compromise policy with the Southern white establishment. Franklin and DuBois were in Georgia on their way to a conference in Atlanta, and they both stopped at one of the few decent hotels available to African Americans at the time. When Franklin saw DuBois sitting and reading a newspaper, he approached his hero and greeted him. DuBois's response was a grunt that dissuaded the **timorous** Franklin from further attempts at communication. Years later, Franklin, now chairman of the history department at a prestigious university, invited DuBois to come to the institution and entertained him over dinner. Franklin then told DuBois of the incident where he felt rebuffed. DuBois apologized and explained that he was an extremely shy or **diffident** person. He didn't mean to be rude but just didn't know what to say when strangers approached him. Thus DuBois acquired the reputation of being aloof or emotionally distant when in reality he had an extreme case of **diffidence**.

8. bona fide (BOH nuh fyd) adj. not counterfeit or phony, genuine
Synonyms: sincere, real,
authentic (aw THEN {"TH" as in "thin"} tik)
Antonym: bogus

Even museums sometimes get tricked when they acquire famous works of art. They might pay a fortune for a presumed masterpiece only to find out that it is an inauthentic copy or a forged document of some historical decree. If even the experts can be fooled into purchasing what they think is a **bona fide** or **authentic** work, we must be extremely careful when someone tries to sell us a work of art or a document that they claim to be **bona fide** but is actually bogus or fake.

HER, HES — stick, cling (hesitate, coherence, adhesive tape)

9. coherent (koh HEER unt) adj. sticking together, logically consistent, easily understood
Related Forms: coherence, coherently
Synonyms: reasonable, comprehensible, intelligible, **cogent** (KOH junt)
Antonyms: incoherent, confused, muddled

10. incoherent (in koh HEER unt) adj. lacking logical connection, hard to understand
Related Forms: incoherence, incoherency, incoherently
Synonyms: disconnected, confused, jumbled, chaotic, incomprehensible, unintelligible, disjointed, **inarticulate** (in ahr TIK yuh lut)
Antonyms: coherent, intelligible, clear, orderly, lucid

The Bible recounts a time when everyone on the earth spoke only one language, so all were **coherent** with each other. However, humans decided to build a tower up to heaven, an act God regarded as prideful and arrogant. God then confused the language of the builders so that they all spoke different languages. Since they were **incoherent** to each other, they could not complete this Tower of Babel. Of course, linguists have theories accounting for the diversity of languages. What happens when one group becomes isolated from another is that after many generations the splinter group develops a new dialect and eventually the two groups speak different languages that are **inarticulate** or incomprehensible to each other. Even when we all speak the same language, we may not always communicate **coherently**. English teachers often point out to students that their essays lack **coherence**. The essays, rather than being **cogent** and logically persuasive, go off track with irrelevant information that only confuses the reader. The worst of the essays are **inarticulate** since they make no sense at all to the reader. However, good writing can be taught and a willing student can learn to shape a **coherent** and **cogently** argued thesis.

WORKING WITH WORDS

UNIT 2, LESSON 3

I. Complete the sentences by using each of the following words once:
perfidy, coherent, matriarchal, diffident, anarchy, incoherent, hierarchy, bona fide, fidelity, monarch

1. Will Rogers (1879-1935)—movie star, radio broadcaster, political commentator, and humorist—was part Cherokee Indian and a ____bona fide____ cowboy who could lasso a scurrying mouse.

2. In Rudyard Kipling's *Jungle Book* about a boy in India raised in the jungle by wolves, the organized wolf society led by a dominant male contrasts with the chaotic ____anarchy____ of the monkeys.

3. Women rule in a ____matriarch____ society.

4. Elizabeth is bold and confident; her sister Joan is shy and ____diffident____ .

5. When you are drunk, you slur your words and your speech becomes ____incoherent____ .

6. My editor corrected a confusing paragraph to make it more ____coherent____ .

7. My friendly coworker told me that he could do little to get me a better position with a higher salary in the corporation since his own status was very low in the organization's ____hierarchy____ .

8. In Shakespeare's *Macbeth*, King Duncan thinks of Macbeth as a loyal subject incapable of performing any act of ____perfidy____, certainly not killing his king.

9. If the lion is the "king of the beasts," he is the ____monarch____ of the animal kingdom.

10. We commonly refer to a dog as man's best friend since a dog is known for its ____fidelity____ and loyalty to its master.

II. This exercise reinforces the difficult synonyms in boldface accompanying the main words derived from word parts. Select the two words that are synonyms.

1.	a. steadfast	b. tricky
	c. faithful	d. swift
2.	a. inarticulate	b. incomprehensible
	c. brilliant	d. cautious
3.	a. chaos	b. belief
	c. nihilism	d. effort
4.	a. fake	b. tasty
	c. real	d. bona fide
5.	a. loud	b. cogent
	c. hateful	d. reasonable
6.	a. matron	b. female supervisor
	c. weapon	d. vehicle
7.	a. brave	b. obvious
	c. timid	d. timorous
8.	a. intelligence	b. duplicity
	c. deceitfulness	d. ignorance
9.	a. ranking	b. punishment
	c. laughter	d. pecking order
10.	a. carriage	b. villain
	c. ruler	d. potentate

UNIT 2
LESSON 4

Prefixes in the following words are underlined.
See page xiv for list of prefixes and their definitions.

Word Parts and Words
HER (stick, cling): inherent, adhere
FA(B) (speak): affable, ineffable, nefarious, infamy
PUG(N) (fight, fist): impugn, repugnant, pugnacious, pugilist

HER, HER — stick, cling (hesitate, coherence, adhesive tape)

11. inherent (in HER unt) adj. existing as a permanent, inseparable, or essential part of something
Related Forms: inherence, inherency, inherently
Synonyms: inborn, natural, basic, essential, innate, **intrinsic** (in TRIN zik)
Antonyms: acquired, extrinsic

"We hold these truths to be self-evident, that all men are created equal, that they are endowed by their creator with certain unalienable rights, that among these are life, liberty and the pursuit of happiness." These lines from the Declaration of Independence, adopted on July 4, 1776, declare that we have certain **inherent** or inalienable rights that cannot rightfully be taken from us. Life, liberty, and the pursuit of happiness are part of our **intrinsic** birthright. Scientists have argued over the centuries about whether heredity or environment has the greater role in determining our characters and personalities. Shakespeare, in his play *The Tempest* about a magician who has been shipwrecked with his daughter on an island for twelve years and subdued its nonhuman inhabitants to his will, addresses this question of nature versus nurture. At one point the magician Prospero describes the creature Caliban, whose mother was a witch, as "A devil, born devil, on whose nature / Nurture can never stick." Prospero thought that heredity or our **inherent** and **intrinsic** natures have a stronger effect in determining our behavior than does our social conditioning.

12. adhere (ad HEER) v. stick firmly
Related Forms: adherence, adherent, adherently
Synonyms: cling, bond, attach, **cohere** (koh HEER)
Antonyms: separate, come apart, come unstuck, fall apart

Greek mythology tells us how the god Prometheus stole fire from Zeus, the king of the gods, to give to mankind. Until this time there were only men on earth. To get even with Prometheus, Zeus fashioned a beautiful woman named Pandora and presented her as a gift to Epimetheus, Prometheus's brother. Prometheus had warned his brother never to accept a gift from Zeus. Epimetheus could not **adhere** to this warning, for he was entranced by Pandora and readily accepted her. With Pandora was a box that the gods had put evils into that would inflict mankind. They warned her never to open the box. Curious Pandora, however, could not resist opening the lid of the box and out flew evils that would plague mankind. Men and women have **cohered** or bonded with each other ever since, but according to this story the blissful life that men had lived up until that time would now be one of hardship and suffering. This Greek story resembles the biblical story that makes Eve the cause of mankind's evils by not **adhering** to God's warning not to eat the fruit of the tree that had been forbidden to them. Perhaps, the stories of Pandora and Eve are a patriarchal society's way of blaming women for the ills of humanity.

FA(B) — speak (fable, famous, infant)

13. affable (AF uh bul) adj. friendly, easy to talk to
Related Forms: affability, affably
Synonyms: sociable, easy going, pleasant, genial, congenial, cordial, **amiable** (AY mee uh bul)
Antonyms: unfriendly, reserved, unapproachable

We think of Santa Claus as jolly, generous, and **affable**. At the beginning of Charles Dickens's tale *A Christmas Carol*, the protagonist greets the oncoming Christmas holiday with a surly, sour, grumbling spirit—the very antithesis of **affability**. He is a miser who resents this holiday of gift-giving and a charitable spirit. However, by the end of the story, after being visited by three supernatural beings who show him his past, present, and possible future, Scrooge is transformed into an **amiable**, joyous, charitable soul.

14. ineffable (in EF uh bul) adj. incapable of being expressed or described in words
Related Forms: ineffability, ineffableness, ineffably
Synonyms: indescribable, inexpressible, **unutterable** (un UT ur uh bul)

"What oft was thought, but ne'er so well expressed." This line from the English poet Alexander Pope (1688-1744) expresses the idea that good writing expresses an idea that we recognize as true though we had never articulated itself to ourselves. However, there are some experiences that are **ineffable** and cannot be put into words. "One picture is worth more than ten thousand words" states the difficulty of words to adequately describe something. In Shakespeare's tragedy *King Lear*, the old King Lear is about to divide his kingdom among his three daughters. All he asks of them is to tell him how much they love him. The hypocritical two eldest daughters have no difficulty in exaggeratingly describing their love. The youngest and sincere Cordelia, put off by the false declarations of her sisters, finds that her love is **unutterable**. King Lear, whose ego is wounded, disowns Cordelia, divides her portion among the other sisters, and eventually suffers terrible misfortune at the hands of his insincere daughters. If he had sensed the **ineffable** love of Cordelia, his miserable fate could have been avoided.

15. nefarious (nih FAIR ee us) adj. very wicked
Related Forms: nefariousness, nefariously
Synonyms: evil, heinous, **iniquitous** (ih NIK wih tus)
Antonyms: good, virtuous

16. infamy (IN fuh mee) n. evil reputation, disgrace
Related Words: infamous, infamously
Synonyms: shame, dishonor, ignominy, iniquity, **notoriety** (noh tuh RY uh tee)
Antonym: honor

We regard Judas and Satan as **nefarious**. Their **iniquitous**, traitorous acts have made them **infamous**, or famous in a bad way. Traditionally, "**notoriety**" has also been used to describe someone who is famous for negative acts. However, "**notoriety**" is now commonly associated with fame, both positive and negative. Call me old-fashioned, but I still don't use the word in relation to a person famed for worthwhile contributions. 1865, the year the Civil War ended, is a famous date in American history. It is also famous in Jamaican history, the year that Jamaican peasants—presumably freed more than two decades earlier by England's abolishment of slavery in their colonies, but who were in reality still treated as slaves—rebelled against their condition. Franklin Emile Halliburton memorialized this event in composing Jamaica's first opera in 2015. Titled *1865*, it dramatizes the brutal suppression of the unsuccessful 1865 rebellion. In this opera there is a famous line where the colonial ruler of the district, on learning of the rebellion, shouts out "**Infamy**!" A chorus of his privileged cohorts echoes this word. They refer to the rebels whom they regard as evil. Of course, the true **infamy** was that of the rulers who **iniquitously** massacred the protestors.

PUG(N) — fight, fist (repugnant)

17. impugn (im PYOON) v. attack or question the truth, goodness, or motive of something

Synonyms: attack, challenge, oppose, **assail** (uh SAYL)

Antonyms: support, defend, advocate, authenticate

Friends, Romans, countrymen, lend me your ears;
I come to bury Caesar, not to praise him.

In Shakespeare's *Julius Caesar*, Brutus and Cassius have just led a group of conspiring senators to assassinate Julius Caesar. Before their blood-soaked daggers have even dried, Brutus had addressed the Roman crowd and explained why Caesar had to be assassinated to prevent him from becoming a dictator. He convinces the crowd of his motives, and they are fully in support of his action. Brutus then makes a fatal mistake. He allows Marc Antony, the dear friend of Caesar, to address the Roman citizenry. Marc Antony then begins his famous speech with the lines quoted above. However, as his speech unfolds, we see his real motive is to praise Caesar and stir up the crowd against Brutus. He does this by stating that "Brutus is an honorable man." Throughout his speech these words are repeated in a subtle and ironic way until finally they come to suggest the opposite of their literal meaning. "Brutus is an honorable man" serves as a refrain that **impugns** the character and motives of Brutus while indeed extolling Caesar. At the conclusion of the speech, Marc Antony has successfully turned the crowd into a mob ready to **assail** or attack Brutus and his followers.

18. repugnant (rih PUG nunt) adj. causing a feeling of strong dislike, disgusting

Related Forms: repugnance, repugnantly

Synonyms: repulsive, distasteful, offensive, detestable, abhorrent, **loathsome** (LOTH sum)

Antonyms: attractive, pleasant

Usually physically **loathsome** monsters have similarly **repugnant** characters and personalities. Outward appearance mirrors inner qualities. But not always. The monster of *Frankenstein, or the Modern Prometheus* (1818) by Mary Shelley, wife of the poet Percy Bysshe Shelley, and the Beast in the fairy tale *Beauty and Beast* have **loathsome** exteriors but inner beauty. The monster in Shelley's novel is never given a name. Later monster films have called him Frankenstein, but the name is actually that of the scientist who created him. Also, the original monster is sensitive, empathic, and yearns to be accepted by society. It is only after he is spurned because of his **loathsome** appearance that his inherent benevolent nature turns to revenge. The Beast in *Beauty and the Beast*, unloved and shunned because of his **repugnant** body, learns to love Beauty who comes to him. Fortunately, she eventually reciprocates the love and thus lifts the spell on this former prince who had been transformed into a monster that others **loathed**. He then becomes a handsome prince once again and all ends happily ever after. Not so for Mary Shelley's monster who has been altered by subsequent works to be both physically and spiritually **repugnant** and **loathsome**.

19. pugnacious (pug NAY shus) adj. inclined to fight or quarrel

Related Forms: pugnaciousness, pugnacity, pugnaciously

Synonyms: combative, quarrelsome, contentious, truculent, bellicose, **belligerent** (buh LIJ uh runt)

Antonyms: peaceful, peaceable

The first scene of Shakespeare's tragedy *Romeo and Juliet* introduces us to the play's most **pugnacious** character—Tybalt. Tybalt is from the Capulet family (as is Juliet) whereas Romeo is a Montague. These families have a history of feuding. In this first scene, Benvolio, a friend of Romeo's, draws his sword in order to stop a fight between the servants of Montague and those of Capulet. When Tybalt joins them, Benvolio explains that he has only drawn his sword to separate and stop the fighting servants. The **belligerent** Tybalt cannot comprehend Benvolio's attempt at making peace. Tybalt tells Benvolio, "What! Drawn, and talk of peace? I hate the word, / As I hate hell, all Montagues and thee." "**Pugnacious**" derives from the Latin word part *pug* meaning "fist, fight," and **belligerent** from the Latin word part *bell* meaning "war," which also gives us the word "bellicose." "**Belligerent**" and "bellicose" are synonymous, both meaning aggressive, hostile, warlike. Certainly, Tybalt exemplifies the qualities of **pugnaciousness**, **belligerence,** and bellicosity.

20. pugilist (PYOO juh lust) n. boxer
Related Forms: pugilism, pugilistic
Synonyms: fighter, prizefighter, clench-fisted
martial (MAR shul) **artist**

When we hear the term **martial** (meaning "warlike, fighting") arts, we usually think of Asian methods of fighting, such as kung fu, tai chi, tae kwon do, karate, judo, and jujitsu. However, one might regard boxing or **pugilism** as the Western **martial** art. Lord Byron (1788-1824), England's satirical poet of the Romantic period who liked to make fun of or assail his adversaries in print, was also intrigued by **pugilism**. Actually, John Jackson who held the British championship in the late eighteenth century, opened a boxing school after he retired. Byron took lessons from him. George Bernard Shaw (1856-1950), one of Great Britain's most prominent playwrights, wrote a youthful novel titled *Cashel Byron's Profession* about a **pugilist** or boxer. An enthusiast of **pugilism**, Shaw called the protagonist of the novel Cashel Byron, paying respect to boxing fan Lord Byron. Later in life, Shaw became friends with the American Gene Tunney, who held the world heavyweight title from 1926-1928 and retired while still holding the championship. Tunney, like Shaw, had an interest in Shakespeare as well as boxing. One of the best-read and literate of boxers, Gene Tunney wrote the article on "Boxing in America" in the 14th edition (1929) of the *Encyclopedia Britannica*. Gene Tunney's son John V. Tunney did not make a career as a prizefighter but could be considered a political **pugilist** as he became U. S. Senator from California.

WORKING WITH WORDS

UNIT 2, LESSONS 3 & 4

The following exercises include all main words derived from word parts and their synonyms in boldface from both Lessons 3 and 4.

1. Match the word on the left with its synonym.

Set 1

___ 1. anarchy	a. duplicity, treason
___ 2. ineffable	b. iniquitous, evil
___ 3. pugnacious	c. loathsome, repulsive
___ 4. nefarious	d. nihilism, chaos
___ 5. perfidy	e. pecking order, ranking
___ 6. repugnant	f. intrinsic, inborn
___ 7. incoherent	g. unutterable, indescribable
___ 8. hierarchy	h. belligerent, quarrelsome
___ 9. bona fide	i. inarticulate, confused
___ 10. inherent	j. authentic, genuine

Set 2

___ 1. monarch	a. notoriety, disgrace
___ 2. coherent	b. cohere, cling
___ 3. affable	c. timorous, shy
___ 4. pugilist	d. potentate, ruler
___ 5. matriarch	e. assail, attack
___ 6. fidelity	f. matron, female leader
___ 7. infamy	g. steadfastness, loyalty
___ 8. adhere	h. cogent, reasonable
___ 9. diffident	i. martial artist, fighter
___ 10. impugn	j. amiable, friendly

II. Complete the sentences by using each of the following words once:

Set 1 Words:
hierarchy, affable, bona fide, pugnacious, adhere, coherent, inherent, impugn, matriarchs, infamy

1. Although I have never lied to the public, my political opponents ________ my honesty.

2. My mother and grandmother are ________ who rule their families.

3. Whereas my father was tolerant, kindly, and always tried to peacefully settle arguments, his ________ brother was ready to punch you if you looked at him the wrong way.

4. President Franklin Delano Roosevelt referred to the Japanese attack on Pearl Harbor on December 7, 1941, as a "date which will live in ________."

5. In our military ________, the generals command the colonels, the colonels command the majors, the majors command the captains, and the captains command the lieutenants.

6. No matter how hard he tried to control his temper, his ________ pugnacious nature would often cause him to get into fights.

7. Our commander told us to ________ to the rules and we would not get in any trouble.

8. I find your lack of logic and imprecise language make it impossible for you to construct a ________ argument.

9. Before you pay thousands of dollars for these autographs of sports heroes, make sure that they are ________ and not fake.

10. Our strict boss is serious, stern, and sometimes even frightening while at work, but once at home with family and friends, he is humorous, lively, and ________.

Set 2 Words:
ineffable, nefarious, anarchy, monarch, diffidence, fidelity, repugnant, incoherent, perfidy, pugilists

1. The opposite of confidence is ____________ .

2. The monarch surrounded himself with advisors who had proven their loyalty, devotion, and ____________ .

3. Joe Louis, Muhammad Ali, and Jack Dempsey were all ____________ .

4. Some people find spiders and snakes ____________ , but I like to observe them and even have them as pets.

5. Perhaps Shakespeare's supreme villain is the ____________ Iago in the play *Othello*; he is intelligent, subtle, thoroughly evil, and utterly without conscience.

6. When the powerful ____________ Alexander the Great approached the philosopher Diogenes and asked if he could do anything for him, the philosopher scornfully replied that the world conqueror could move a little since he was blocking the sun.

7. The dictator rose to power since he restored order to the country where previously there was only chaos, disorder, and ____________ .

8. The experience of the enchanted forest with its heavenly sounds was ____________ or impossible to describe in words.

9. In Shakespeare's play *Julius Caesar*, Julius Caesar is shocked at the ____________ of Brutus; he had loved Brutus who now stabs him as one of the conspirators in his assassination.

10. Stop your ____________ babbling, organize your thoughts, and make sense when you speak.

III. *HEART OF DARKNESS, THINGS FALL APART, THE ANALECTS*: ANARCHY AND ORDER

Fill in each blank by using each of the following only once:

Set 1 Words:
bona fide, nefarious, incoherent, perfidious, infamy, pugnacious, impugn, repugnant, pugilist, ineffable

Heart of Darkness by the English writer Joseph Conrad (1857-1924), *Things Fall Apart* by the Nigerian Chinua Achebe (1939-2013), and the *Analects* of the ancient Chinese philosopher Confucius (551-479 B.C.) depict societies struggling to maintain order as anarchic forces crack their foundations. Joseph Conrad was born in Poland, migrated to France, and only came to England when he was in his twenties. English being his third language, he eventually became a master stylist of English prose. Remarkably, he became a writer after a career of twenty years as a seaman on merchant ships that sailed to such places as East Asia, India, Australia, South America, and Africa. In the 1890s, Conrad was a seaman on a steam ship that traveled Africa's Congo River, a journey much like that described in his story *Heart of Darkness*.

Heart of Darkness scathingly portrays the ______________, evil, or wicked abuses of colonialism at that time in the Belgian Congo. The story for the most part is narrated by Marlow, who has been hired to take a steamboat and reach a distant ivory outpost controlled by a man named Kurtz. On his journey, Marlow witnesses how Africans have been turned into living skeletons as the colonialists have used them as slave labor. Kurtz was unusual in that he came not primarily out of profit motives but out of idealism to educate and enlighten the native Africans to Western civilization. However, the great irony is that his ideals have undergone a ______________ or treacherous transformation. In one of Kurtz's manuscripts on bringing the light and goodness of Western civilization to the Africans, Marlow discovers a note on the last page, “Exterminate all the brutes.” Marlow struggles to understand the meaning of Kurtz's at times ____________, confused ramblings. Kurtz, the idealist representing the glory of Western civilization, has succumbed to his environment and given in to the temptation to be a god-like leader to the natives. Power and greed have consumed him. Kurtz's last words are, "The horror! The horror!" Perhaps he has looked into the depths of his own soul and witnessed its perfidious betrayal to his ideals. Conrad is showing what Europeans considered the "heart of darkness," the unknown regions in Africa's interior, is only one form of darkness. The deeper darkness is that within the inhabitants of the so-called civilized nations; they have manifested the ____________ or extreme disgrace and shame of giving in to greed and ravenous exploitation in their conquest of the planet. The true heart of darkness lies buried beneath the glossy veneer of civilization on which the colonists pride themselves. Conrad struggles to present us with his vision of humanity but perhaps shares the viewpoint of his narrator Marlow, "No, it is impossible; it is impossible to convey the life-sensation of any given epoch of one's existence—that which makes its truth, its meaning—its subtle and penetrating essence. It is impossible. We live, as we dream—alone." Ultimately one's vision may be ____________ or inexpressible, unable to be transmitted into words. Conrad's often at times complex, confusing, richly symbolic tale *Heart of Darkness* heroically wrestles to communicate an ineffable experience that exceeds the words that try to grasp it.

Whereas Joseph Conrad condemns the European exploitation of Africa, he fails to individualize the Africans or have the reader share their viewpoint. The Nigerian Chinua Achebe shows the invasion of Western civilization into a traditional Nigerian village during roughly the same time period as Conrad's *Heart of Darkness*. However, Achebe shows this encounter from the perspective of the Africans. The protagonist of the novel *Things Fall Apart* is Okonkwo. As a young man he brings honor to his village as a great fighter—not as a ____________ or boxer that might be common in the West, but as a wrestler, the traditional manly sport of his village. He becomes a ____________ or genuine sports hero who is undefeated in wrestling contests for seven years. Okonkwo's father was lazy, carefree, and a failure. In reaction to his father whose qualities Okonkwo found ____________ or disgusting and repulsive, Okonkwo becomes extremely industrious, conscientious, and stern—qualities he thinks manly in contrast to what he regarded as effeminate weaknesses in his father. Okonkwo could be ____________ or combative and belligerent and would not hesitate to beat his wives if he felt justified. Through a tragic accident, his rifle goes off during a festival and accidentally kills a fellow villager. He is thus banished from his village for seven years. Upon returning to his home village, he finds much changed. Christian missionaries have become influential and traditions are weakening. Conflict between some of the villages and the new uncompromising missionary results in the church being burned to the ground. The District Commissioner summons six of the leaders of the village to discuss matters with him, Okonkwo being one of the leaders. However, once within the District Commissioner's confines, the African leaders are humiliated, their heads shaved, and they are beaten with sticks. After Okonkwo and the others are allowed to return to their village, five messengers from the white man's court visit them. Infuriated, Okonkwo takes his machete and severs the chief messenger's head from his body. His villagers do not go to war to support him and Okonkwo ends his life by hanging himself. *Things Fall Apart* shows in great detail the daily activities, interactions, and customs of a Nigerian village. We learn about them as individuals and can understand their viewpoints. However, their way of life disintegrates as Western civilization infiltrates. Although Achebe equably does not portray either the villagers or the European colonizers as either all good or bad, *Things Fall Apart* does ____________ or attack the lack of understanding of the Westerners of the African villages that results in the crumbling of traditions that causes native communities to fall apart.

Set 2 Words:
matriarchy, diffidence, inherent, hierarchy, affability, adhere, anarchy, monarch, cohering, fidelity

Both Conrad and Achebe describe societies whose structures are no longer ____________ or sticking together to keep the societies in harmonious organization. Western influences are unraveling traditional village life in *Things Fall Apart*. *Heart of Darkness* portrays the European plundering and destruction of Africans but also shows that the West's corruption of its ideals, as it gives in to its greedy impulses, is destroying the fabric of its own civilization. How to maintain a healthy order that fends off ____________ or disorder and the breakdown of society has been a perennial question for humans.

Over two thousand years before Conrad and Achebe, China's Confucius explored this concern. The philosopher Confucius viewed China as degenerating from an earlier dynasty where the ____________ or ruler established order and justice. Now warlords were gaining power and their continuous fighting amongst themselves threatened to tear apart the fabric of Chinese civilization. Confucius was a teacher who hoped to establish a structure by which harmony could be restored to his country. The *Analects* is a collection of Confucius's sayings, proverbs, and guidelines by his disciples that came to have an enormous influence on China.

Confucius did not think of human beings having strong ____________ or inborn qualities of good or evil; rather, he thought that basically our inherent nature is flexibleness or capability of being changed or molded. He believed that tradition, custom, and ritual could shape individuals and their relationships with each other into a harmonious society. For example, Confucius counseled that there should be proper relations between parent and child, husband and wife, older and younger sibling, older and younger friend, and ruler and subject. The elder or more powerful party should be loving, patient, kind, and attentive. Children, wives, younger siblings, and friends should show proper respect, reverence, and obedience. Whereas monarchs should be generous and just, their subjects should demonstrate ____________ or loyalty. If everyone performed their role within this ____________ or gradation of relationships, a good family life would extend itself into a good nation. Of course, the hierarchy was tilted toward the male and not a ____________ or rule by women since husbands were dominant over wives and sons prized over daughters. One of Confucius's main principles was that we should not wish on others what we would not wish done to ourselves. Values and relationships would ____________ or stick firmly through means of conscious attention to traditions and customs. Respect for oneself and others would instill confidence and not ____________ or timidity in knowing and acting the correct way. A dignified ____________ or friendliness would permeate the nation. Thus, the proper social relations between individuals would establish order in society so civilization would not fall apart.

UNIT 3
LESSON 5

Prefixes in the following words are underlined.
See page xiv for list of prefixes and their definitions.

Word Parts and Words
SPEC, SPIC (look): specious, conspicuous, auspicious, circumspect
LUD, LUS (play): elusive, allude, collusion, ludicrous
PEND, PENS (hang, weigh, pay): pensive, propensity, compensate, impending
SAL, SIL, SULT (leap, jump): desultory, salient, resilient, sally
POT (power): potent, impotent, omnipotent, potentate

1. specious (SPEE shus) adj. seemingly true or correct but actually incorrect, wrong, or false
Related Forms: speciousness, speciously
Synonyms: misleading, deceptive, spurious, **fallacious** (fuh LAY shus)
Antonyms: valid, logical

Clever arguments can sometimes persuade, even if the reasoning may be somewhat faulty. In ancient Greece, some men were paid huge sums to teach their clients how to win cases in courts or persuade the public to vote them into office. For these teachers, who were called Sophists, the goal was winning; it did not matter whether the reasoning was **specious** as long as it successfully convinced. Enemies of the ancient Greek philosopher Socrates accused him of being a Sophist. Socrates defended himself against this charge during a trial accusing him of not believing in the state's official gods and corrupting the youth of Athens. Socrates showed that unlike the Sophists he never took money for his teaching and was only concerned with the truth rather than with teaching how to win victories in court or politics. Unfortunately, even though Socrates showed the **specious** and **fallacious** reasoning of his accusers, emotion prevailed over reason and the court sentenced Socrates to death.

2. conspicuous (kun SPIK yoo us) adj. easily seen, very noticeable, attracting attention

Related Forms: conspicuousness, conspicuously

Synonyms: obvious, apparent, visible, outstanding, prominent, clearly **discernible** (dih SUR nuh bul)

Antonyms: inconspicuous, hidden, indistinct

Whether it's designer clothes or mansions, people like to display their wealth to others. Even though some can barely afford it, they want to **conspicuously** demonstrate the appearance of financial success. Individuals who cannot afford a luxury car may even pool their money so that they can share the car and be **discernible** to others as having a higher economic status than they do in reality. The American economist Thorstein Veblen coined the term "**conspicuous** consumption" in his treatise *The Theory of the Leisure Class* (1899) to describe how the wealthy prominently display their luxury for prestige. In the animal kingdom, male birds like the peacock elaborately parade their colorful plumage to attract mates. Of course, the coloring of many animals blends in with their surroundings so that they will be inconspicuous or not stand out and be clearly **discernible** to other animals that want to eat them.

3. auspicious (aw SPISH us) adj. favorable, promising a good outcome

Related Forms: auspiciousness, auspiciously

Synonyms: promising, encouraging, **propitious** (pruh PISH us)

Antonyms: inauspicious, ill-omened, unpromising, unfavorable

"**Auspicious**" derives from the Latin *avis* meaning "bird," and *specio* meaning "look, see." The ancient Romans looked to the flight of birds and even dissected birds to see signs of the future. Favorable or **auspicious** interpretations would decide when it was best to initiate an important event, such as a war. Of course, if the signs were inauspicious or unfavorable, action would be forestalled. Some people go to fortune tellers who read their palms, look into a crystal ball, or read tea leaves to tell them of **auspicious** or **propitious** events like finding the love of their lives, gaining entrance to the university of their choice, or obtaining a lucrative and satisfying job. Whereas an **auspicious** forecast fills one with joy, an inauspicious prediction can cause dread.

4. circumspect (SUR kum spekt) adj. cautious, careful
Related Forms: circumspection, circumspectly
Synonyms: watchful, attentive, heedful, wary,
prudent (PROOD unt)
Antonyms: unguarded, unwary, careless

An ancient Greek myth tells how the hero Perseus succeeded in his mission to find Medusa, a hideous monster with braids of hissing snakes for hair, and bring back her head. Anyone who looked directly upon the Medusa would turn to stone. With the aid of a magic cap that made him invisible, Perseus was most **circumspect** in approaching Medusa so as to avoid detection. Also, he was extremely **prudent** or careful in only looking at her reflection in a polished shield. He managed to approach her, use his sword to decapitate her, and returned with her head that turned his enemies to stone.

LUD, LUS — play (delude, interlude, illusion)

5. elusive (ih LOO siv) adj. hard to grasp or pin down
Related Forms: elusiveness, elusively
Synonyms: baffling, slippery, **evasive** (ih VAY siv)

In Greek mythology Atalanta, though a woman, was an outstanding hunter and runner. In fact, she could outrun any man. Therefore, when her father pressured her to get married—Atalanta wanted to remain a virgin—she agreed on the condition that she would marry the man who could beat her in a foot race. She always gave her suitor a head start, but then caught up with him and thrust a spear through his back. In this way she **eluded** or avoided marriage, since her suitors could not **evade** her. However, Aphrodite, goddess of love, gave one suitor three golden apples. As Atalanta was catching up with him, he threw one of the apples and Atalanta, sure that she could catch him, veered to the side, picked up the apple, and then proceeded to gain on her opponent. Then the suitor tossed the second apple with the same results. Atalanta scooped up this apple and approached her rival with the finish line in sight. He dropped the third apple. Atalanta miscalculated, thinking she could get the apple and the victory. Thus, the suitor proved too **elusive** to catch, **evaded** her spear, and won her for his wife. In political races, politicians, when asked specific questions, sometimes give **evasive** answers; they are too **elusive** to be committed to any definite policy or course of action.

6. allude (uh LOOD) v. refer indirectly
Related Form: allusion
Synonyms: suggest, hint at, **imply** (im PLY)

If we say "a rose by any other name would smell as sweet" or "to be or not to be, that is the question," we are making **allusions** to Shakespeare's plays. The first quotation **alludes** to *Romeo and Juliet*, the second to *Hamlet*. There are famous **allusions** from history as well as from literature. Henry II, a twelfth century king of England, had been trying to gain control of the Church in England. He thought that by appointing his friend Thomas Beckett as the Archbishop of Canterbury, the highest church official in England, he would achieve his goal. However, Beckett gave his allegiance to the Church and Pope rather than to Henry. Thwarted by Beckett, Henry presumably shouted out in court, "Will no one rid me of this meddlesome priest?" Four knights took the words as **alluding** to Beckett, as **implying** that the king wanted Beckett dead. Acting on this **allusion**, they murdered the archbishop in his cathedral at Canterbury. Beckett became a martyr, saint, and his church a shrine. It became a site for pilgrimages. The pilgrims in Chaucer's *The Canterbury Tales* journey from London to this shrine in Canterbury.

7. collusion (kuh LOO zhun) n. secret agreement or cooperation for a wrong, dishonest, or illegal purpose
Related Forms: colluder, collude, collusive, collusively
Synonyms: plotting, scheming, connivance, complicity, **conspiracy** (kun SPIR uh see)

Aaron Burr narrowly missed being President of the United States. In 1800 he tied with Thomas Jefferson for the number of votes from the Electoral College that determines the presidency. The House of Representatives then determined who would be president by electing Jefferson. At that time, the candidate in second place become vice president, so Burr assumed this office under Jefferson. However, we generally associate Burr with scandal. He challenged Alexander Hamilton to a duel and killed Hamilton, who was the first Secretary of the Treasury, a founding father of the United States, and whose face appears on the ten-dollar bill. Thomas Jefferson also ordered Burr arrested for **colluding** to detach a part of the United States for his personal gain. Burr was tried for this **conspiracy** but was acquitted of the charge of treason in 1807.

8. ludicrous (LOO dih krus) adj. laughably ridiculous
Related Forms: ludicrousness, ludicrously
Synonyms: ridiculous, foolish, silly, absurd, **preposterous** (prih POS tur us)
Antonyms: sensible, serious, solemn

The Bible recounts how three angels told Abraham that he would have a son by his wife Sarah. Sarah overheard the messengers and laughed, since she was well past the time of menopause. She thought it **ludicrous** that she would conceive. Nevertheless, within about a year—when Abraham was 100 and Sarah 90—the **preposterous** became possible as she gave birth to Isaac. "Isaac" means "he laughs," a fitting name for one whose birth seemed so **ludicrous** and **preposterous**.

PEND, PENS — hang, weigh, pay
(depend, suspend, suspense, expense)

9. pensive (PEN siv) adj. quietly thoughtful, sometimes in a sad or dreamy way
Related Forms: pensiveness, pensively
Synonyms: reflective, meditative,
contemplative (kun TEM pluh tiv, KUN tum play tiv)
Antonym: unreflective

"Once upon a midnight dreary, while I pondered weak and weary" begins Edgar Allan Poe's poem "The Raven." The narrator of the poem is in a **pensive** or **contemplative** mood as he is remembering and mourning the death of his lover, Lenore. A raven appears and to all the narrator's questions, it answers with the refrain "nevermore." The poem's rocking rhythm and repetitive rhyme contribute to evoking a mood of mystery and an almost supernatural dread as the initial **pensive** mood of the lost lover Lenore becomes intensified to a dread that the pain of loss will never be lifted from his soul. Published in 1845, "The Raven" brought Poe instant fame. In an essay, Poe explained how he pondered or **contemplated** a long time before he created the poem. He makes it clear that the rhyme, rhythm, refrain, and subject matter were the result of his **contemplation** and **pensive** planning so that the construction of the poem was not one of unconscious inspiration but as carefully developed as a mathematical proof. One of America's greatest writers, Edgar Allan Poe not only composed poems but also was a pioneer in the detective story and tales of horror and the supernatural.

10. propensity (pruh PEN sih tee) n. natural tendency or inclination
Synonyms: leaning, preference, predisposition, penchant, proclivity, **predilection** (pred uh LEK shun)
Antonyms: disinclination, aversion

The Austrian Wolfgang Amadeus Mozart (1756-1791), a supreme genius among musical composers, revealed a **propensity** for music early in life. He played a keyboard instrument at four and was composing by five. In fact, his **predilection** for music was so strong that as a boy he would choose to remain at the keyboard for many hours until his father forced him to quit. For all his **propensity** and proclivity that developed to produce symphonies, church music, and such operatic masterpieces as *The Marriage of Figaro*, *Don Giovanni*, and *The Magic Flute*, Mozart had difficulties supporting his family and died in poverty so that his corpse was placed in a common vault receiving about twenty other paupers, and no stone or cross signified the place of his remains.

WORKING WITH WORDS

UNIT 3, LESSON 5

I. Complete the sentences by using each of the following words once:
auspicious, collusion, circumspect, pensive, specious, elusive, propensity, conspicuous, allude, ludicrous

1. The great American athlete Jim Thorpe showed a propensity for sports at an early age.

2. We find it difficult to tackle the elusive football runner who is as slippery as an eel.

3. His argument may persuade many people but I find it faulty and specious.

4. The enormous mole on her face is conspicuous.

5. At one time people thought the earth was flat and if you walked to the edge you would fall off; today that idea seems ludicrous.

6. We did not want to disturb her serious and pensive mood while she was deciding if she should accept a job offer in another country.

7. The blue, cloudless sky, delightful breeze, and pleasant temperature signified an auspicious day for an outdoor graduation ceremony.

8. When people speak of robbing the rich to give to the poor, they allude to the activities of Robin Hood.

9. My mechanic friend makes a circumspect examination of any used car he considers purchasing, checking carefully the tires, engine, brakes, and steering.

10. The bank officials were guilty of collusion in cheating investors by falsifying the stated profits.

II. This exercise reinforces the difficult synonyms in boldface accompanying the main words derived from word parts. Select the two words that are synonyms.

1. a. wicked b. terrifying
c. favorable d. propitious

2. a. preposterous b. absurd
c. intelligent d. careful

3. a. false b. thoughtful
c. fallacious d. accident prone

4. a. luck b. misfortune
c. predilection d. preference

5. a. hidden b. discernible
c. noticeable d. blind

6. a. thoughtful b. contemplative
c. imaginative d. worried

7. a. careful b. bold
c. timid d. prudent

8. a. conspiracy b. careful observation
c. scheming d. disaster

9. a. evasive b. slippery
c. carefree d. dynamic

10. a. threaten b. capture
c. imply d. suggest

UNIT 3
LESSON 6

Prefixes in the following words are underlined.
See page xiv for list of prefixes and their definitions.

Word Parts and Words
PEND, PENS (hang, weigh, pay): compensate, impending
SAL, SIL, SULT (leap, jump): desultory, salient, resilient, sally
POT (power): potent, impotent, omnipotent, potentate

11. compensate (KOM pun sayt) v. make up for, pay
Related Forms: compensation, compensatory
Synonyms: balance, counterbalance, offset, counteract, repay, **reimburse** (ree im BURS)

Who enjoys the act of making love more, the man or the woman? Zeus, the King of the Greek gods, and his queen, Hera, were debating this question. Zeus thought the woman received the greater pleasure, Hera thought the man. To get the answer, they summoned Tiresias. As a young man, Tiresias had come upon two snakes entwined in the sexual act. He killed the female. For this he was turned into a woman. Seven years later he came upon two snakes similarly engaged and this time killed the male. Tiresias was transformed back into a man. Since he had experience as both a man and woman, he was chosen by the gods to solve the debate. He sided with Zeus. Enraged, Hera blinded him. Zeus **compensated** Tiresias for this loss by giving him the prophetic gift of foresight and an extremely long life. A medieval European legend of the Pied Piper who came to the German town of Hamlin concerns withholding **compensation**. The mayor of Hamlin promised the Pied Piper that he would richly reward him if he freed the town from rats. Luring the rats with the music of his magic pipe, he brought them to a river where they drowned. However, the town failed to **reimburse** the Pied Piper the promised fee. He left in anger but returned in disguise to enchant the children of the town with his flute and led them away, never to return. Both Tiresias and the Pied Piper suffered after performing their tasks; Tiresias was **compensated** with the gift of prophecy whereas the Pied Piper **reimbursed** or paid back the town with vengeance.

12. impending (im PEND ing) adj. about to happen, occur, or appear soon
Synonyms: coming, nearing, approaching, forthcoming, looming, **imminent** (IM uh nunt)

In ancient Greece, Damocles, who served at the court of the dictator Dionysus, constantly praised this powerful ruler as the happiest of men. One day Dionysus sat Damocles down at a table for a sumptuous feast. Damocles was enjoying himself immensely. Then Dionysus pointed to a sword that dangled from a thin thread directly over Damocles head. Dionysus was implying that a monarch, no matter how powerful and magnificent, faced **imminent** death. The threat of **impending** doom was a constant anxiety in the mind of a dictator. The expression "sword of Damocles" has come to mean "**imminent** peril, constantly threatening danger."

SAL, SIL, SULT — leap, jump (salmon, insult, result)

13. desultory (DES ul tor ee) adj. random, unmethodical, aimless
Related Forms: desultoriness, desultorily
Synonyms: irregular, unsystematic, unplanned, rambling, **haphazard** (hap HAZ urd)
Antonyms: orderly, systematic, methodical, purposeful, focused

Trick riders in ancient Roman circuses that leaped from one horse to another were *desultors*, from Latin *salire* (jump, leap) and *de* (from). Some scholars say that "salmon" derives from *salire* as well. Salmon are born in fresh water, leave for the sea, and then return to the place of their birth in order to spawn or reproduce. On their return journey, salmon will leap up to ten feet to overcome waterfalls. Of course, the Roman acrobats were skillfully focused and precise; the salmon are definite and determined as they hone in on the target of their birthplace. Contrarily, if someone is a **desultory** reader, they are far from focused, randomly jumping from one subject or book to another. One becomes an outstanding scholar or athlete not by **desultory** study or **haphazard** training but by dedicated, persistent effort according to a specific program.

14. salient (SAY lee unt) adj. very noticeable, strikingly obvious and attracting attention
Related Forms: salience, saliently
Synonyms: noticeable, noteworthy, outstanding, obvious, prominent, extremely **conspicuous** (kun SPIK yoo us)
Antonym: inconspicuous

In the play *Cyrano de Bergerac* by the Frenchman Edmond Rostand (1868-1918), the main character Cyrano has an extraordinarily large nose. When someone insults him by saying his nose is very big, Cyrano responds that the insulter might have been more imaginative about describing this **salient** feature. Cyrano suggests that his nose could have been referred to as a perch for birds, a rack to hang a hat on, or a spear on his face to defend against charging soldiers. These descriptions more colorfully describe his most **conspicuous** nose. There have been several film versions of this play if you want to see this **salient** trait of Cyrano's face. In the story about the puppet who turned into a little boy, the puppet Pinocchio's nose lengthens as he lies, making it extraordinarily **conspicuous** when he tells a falsehood. One of the most prominent noses in the animal kingdom is that of the elephant. The elephant's trunk is a combination of his upper lip and nose. This **salient** trunk can be about five feet in length and pick up a six-hundred pound log as well as a tiny coin.

15. resilient (rih ZIL yunt) adj. able to resume shape; recovering or adjusting quickly after an illness or setback
Related Forms: resilience, resiliency, resiliently
Synonyms: elastic, adjustable, flexible, responsive, adaptable, **buoyant** (BOY unt)
Antonyms: inflexible, rigid, unaccommodating, unresponsive

Exuberance, energy, activity characterized President Theodore "Teddy" Roosevelt (1858-1919). As a child he was weak, sickly, asthmatic, and short-sighted. Nevertheless, he had the **resilience** to restore himself to physical health and acquire strength. When as a boy his weakness made him the target of bullies, he learned how to box, eventually was on Harvard's championship boxing team, and continued to spar with professional pugilists even when in the White House. Tragedy struck when on February 14th, 1884, both his wife and mother died. Roosevelt's **resilient** and **buoyant** nature helped him recover from this terrible loss. After having served as president from 1901-1909, Roosevelt decided in 1912 to again run for the presidency. About to give a campaign speech, he was shot. The **resilient** Roosevelt, with a bullet lodged in his bloody chest, nevertheless continued to give his speech, although he eventually lost the election. His **resilience** and **buoyancy** in physical activities, politics, and personal relationships made him an extremely popular figure as still evidenced by the stuffed animal that stemmed from his nickname—the teddy bear.

16. sally (SAL ee) n. sudden onslaught, attack, or rush forward; clever or witty remark or comeback

Synonyms: charge, raid, attack, assault, foray, **incursion** (in KUR zhun)

Antonym: retreat

Theirs not to make reply,
Theirs not to reason why,
Theirs but to do and die.
Into the valley of Death
Rode the six hundred.

These lines from the poem "The Charge of the Light Brigade" by England's Alfred, Lord Tennyson commemorate the **sally** of six hundred British cavalry charging Russian artillery in the Crimean War in 1854. Crimea is a peninsula just to the south of Ukraine. The British horsemen strongly suspected that the orders must be a mistake since the sudden **incursion** was clearly a suicide mission. Nevertheless, they faithfully followed orders, rushed forward, and lost three-fourths of their men. Shortly after this **sally**, Tennyson wrote his poem as a tribute to the loyalty and bravery of this British cavalry that **sallied** to their death.

POT — power (potential)

17. potent (POH tunt) adj. powerful, effective
Related Forms: potency, potently
Synonyms: strong, mighty, effectual, **efficacious** (ef uh KAY shus)
Antonyms: impotent, weak, ineffectual, ineffective

18. impotent (IM puh tunt) adj. powerless, helpless, ineffective, (of a male) incapable of sexual intercourse
Related Forms: impotence, impotency, impotently
Synonyms: weak, inadequate, incapable, useless, **ineffectual** (in uh FEK choo ul)
Antonyms: potent, powerful, effective

What is about an inch or two in length, weighs around one ounce, is brightly colored, and has enough poison to kill ten men? In Central and South America live tiny frogs whose skin secretes a most **potent** poison. These poison dart frogs got their name from the native hunters who would use the frog's poison to tip the darts of their blowguns. Although the poison can kill a human within three minutes, a species of snake has evolved to develop an **efficacious** or effective immunity to the frog's toxin so as to render it **impotent** or **ineffectual**.

19. omnipotent (ahm NIP uh tunt) adj. all-powerful
Related Form: omnipotence
Synonyms: almighty, supreme, **preeminent** (pree EM uh nunt)
Antonym: powerless

20. potentate (POHT un tayt) n. powerful ruler, powerful or dominant leader
Synonyms: ruler, monarch, **sovereign** (SAHV run)

In the monotheistic religions (Judaism, Christianity, and Islam) God is thought of as **omnipotent** and omniscient (from Latin *omnis* meaning "all" and *scire* meaning "know") or all-knowing. This concept of God differs from the way ancient Greeks thought of their most mighty god, Zeus. Although Zeus was the **potentate** or ruler who was preeminent or supreme among the Greek gods, he was powerful but not **omnipotent**; he could not avoid the destiny decreed by the Fates. Also the **sovereign** Zeus was not omniscient since he was not aware of everything and could even be fooled by his wife, Hera. For Jews, Christians, and Muslims—unlike the ancient Greeks who believed in many gods—there is only one God who is **preeminently** omniscient and **omnipotent**.

WORKING WITH WORDS

UNIT 3, LESSONS 5 & 6

The following exercises include all main words derived from word parts and their synonyms in boldface from both Lessons 5 and 6.

1. Match the word on the left with its synonym.

Set 1

___ 1. auspicious	a. conspiracy, scheming
___ 2. potentate	b. reimburse, repay
___ 3. collusion	c. buoyant, adjustable
___ 4. conspicuous	d. evasive, slippery
___ 5. compensate	e. imminent, coming
___ 6. desultory	f. sovereign, monarch
___ 7. resilient	g. discernible, obvious
___ 8. elusive	h. contemplative, meditative
___ 9. pensive	i. propitious, favorable
___ 10. impending	j. haphazard, unsystematic

Set 2

___ 1. salient	a. imply, suggest
___ 2. circumspect	b. preposterous, absurd
___ 3. allude	c. fallacious, deceptive
___ 4. propensity	d. prudent, watchful
___ 5. potent	e. incursion, attack
___ 6. sally	f. ineffectual, useless
___ 7. specious	g. efficacious, effectual
___ 8. omnipotent	h. conspicuous, outstanding
___ 9. ludicrous	i. preeminent, all-mighty
___ 10. impotent	j. predilection, inclination

II. Complete the following sentences by using each of the following words only once:

Set 1 Words:

elusive, compensate, impotent, specious, conspicuous, propensity, desultory, resilient, collude, omnipotent

1. You must change your ____________ study habits; concentrate and focus.

2. Do students ____________ to cheat on examinations?

3. Because the father could not swim, he felt ____________ as he watched from the shore as his son drowned.

4. The mouse was too ____________ for us to catch.

5. Some action heroes may have superpowers, but only God is ____________.

6. If sight is lost, other senses like hearing and touch ____________ by becoming more sensitive.

7. Be cautious of clever speakers whose reasoning sounds persuasive but is ____________.

8. If you stretch a ____________ rubber band and then let go, it will resume its original shape.

9. Since Pamela has a ____________ for mathematics, she might become an accountant, statistician, or physicist.

10. Henry felt embarrassed by the ____________ ketchup stain on his white shirt.

Set 2 Words:
salient, ludicrous, impending, sally, potentate, circumspect, pensive, auspicious, allude, potent

1. We resisted the ____________ of the enemy troops.

2. Our grandmother grew ____________ as we asked her to recall what it was like when, as a young woman, she came to this country as an immigrant.

3. The ____________ feature of the giraffe is its long neck.

4. The chairman feasted and praised the visiting ____________ since the chairman wanted to complete a trade deal with the visitor.

5. Be ____________ and inspect a house carefully before you actually purchase it.

6. Stories often introduce a darkening sky, cawing ravens, howls of wolves, and distant shrieks to herald an ____________ horror.

7. Antibiotics are ____________ drugs in treating bacterial infections.

8. At one time Hercules had to serve as a slave to Queen Omphale who made him appear ____________ when she dressed him in women's clothes.

9. I would rather that you do not hint or ____________ to my faults but tell me specifically what they are so that I can correct them.

10. Blue skies, gentle breezes, and a pleasantly warm temperature were ____________ signs that this day would be good for a picnic.

III. DOUBT AND CERTAINTY: DESCARTES AND AL-GHAZALI
Fill in each blank by using each of the following only once:

Set 1 Words:

pensive, desultory, potent, sallies, circumspect, propensity, salient, auspicious, collusion, elusive

What can I know for sure, and what is the true meaning of things? These questions absorbed, or more accurately obsessed, the French philosopher, scientist, and mathematician Rene Descartes (1597-1650) and the Muslim philosopher, theologian, and mystic Al-Ghazali (1058-1111). These two, driven by their powerful ______________ or natural inclination to search for what is indisputably real and true, applied their ______________ or powerful intellects to resolve their doubt and discover certainty. They engaged in effective intellectual ______________ or attacks on specious or faulty reasoning in their unrelenting pursuit of truth.

A ____________________ or thoughtful individual, Descartes tells us that on a day that proved ______________ or extremely favorable, he was able to shut himself away from the cold in a stove-heated room and there conceived of a method that he could apply to philosophy. In his works *Discourse on Method* and *Meditations on First Philosophy*, Descartes applies this method of focused, systematic, analytical reasoning—never lapsing into ______________ or aimless and random thinking—to grasp the ______________ or slippery source of certainty. He states that information through the senses is unreliable. This is readily apparent when we look at a straight stick in water and it appears bent or when the immense distant stars seem to be tiny specks of light. Descartes shows that dreams that seem so real while we are dreaming seem less so upon our awakening. He then speculates that what we take for normal, waking reality may be in fact an illusion created by a demon to deceive us. Thus the senses, dreams, and even this supposed demon all are in _____________ or dishonest cooperation to prevent us from discovering what is truly real. At this point, Descartes says that __________ or careful reasoning has shown him that it is possible to doubt everything. Well, almost everything.

Descartes points out that there is one _____________ or strikingly obvious exception. Doubt itself exists. Descartes then says that since doubt exists, there must be an entity who is a doubter. From this line of reasoning, Descartes reaches his famous conclusion, "I think, therefore I am." Thus he discovers the certainty of his own existence. From this foundation, Descartes then proceeds to show what other things we can be sure of. From a modern perspective, we may say that all the thought of doubt shows us for certain is that the thought of doubt exists. Whether there is a substance or essence that is an "I" that perceives the doubter may still be uncertain. For could not this "I" just be another thought? If there is indeed a substantial observer that is aware, who or what has observed this observer? Thus, the source of awareness can be continuously traced back without ever reaching a fixed identity of an entity that is an observer. Modern brain scientists tell us that there is no fixed point that is an observer in our brains; rather awareness is a process that arises from the interactions of the neurons in our brains. Perhaps this sounds confusing and even irrelevant; however, mystics or those who experience, not just intellectually comprehend, the ultimate source of reality as posited in the world's major religions, often declare that all that exists is consciousness itself, pure awareness from which a sense of both observer and observed have disappeared. From this experience, the sense of a separate, distinct, personal "I" has vanished, and there is no longer the desire to be in conflict with others since the mystic now empathizes with all beings as part of the same reality. If these statements seem confusing, it may be unavoidable. Descriptions of what is ultimately real may always remain paradoxical or contradictory, unable to be contained by language or proven by logic.

Set 2 Words:
potentate, specious, compensate, ludicrous, omnipotent, conspicuous, resiliency, impending, allude, impotent

Over five hundred years before Descartes, the Muslim mystic Al-Ghazali struggled with doubt in many ways similar to that of Descartes. Al-Ghazali was one of the foremost scholars in the Islamic tradition. The religion of Islam shares many similarities with Judaism and Christianity. Of these three monotheistic religions, Judaism is the earliest. Christianity branched off from Judaism when the followers of Jesus, himself a Jew, regarded him as divine. About six hundred years after Jesus, Muhammad had his revelation that led to the formation of Islam. Judaism, Christianity, and Islam are all monotheistic; all express a belief in only one omniscient (all-knowing) and __________ or all-powerful God. Likewise, if someone would ______________ or refer to the first man and woman, followers of all three religions would know that the reference was to Adam and Eve. The Koran, the sacred text of Islam, shares the same early history recounted in the Bible. The Bible and Koran trace the human heritage from Adam to Abraham. But whereas the Bible follows the story of Abraham's son Isaac, the Koran emphasizes those descended from Abraham's son Ishmael. Both Jews and Muslims do not accept the divinity of Jesus, but Muslims revere him as a prophet and even believe in his virgin birth. Thus we can see that although the three religions differ, they may be regarded as cousins in a common spiritual tradition. Muslim practice may be summarized in the Five Pillars of Islam. The first pillar is Islam's creed, "There is no God but Allah, and Muhammad is his prophet." Since "Allah" literally means "the God," this creed merely asserts the shared belief with Jews and Christians in only one God. For Muslims, however, Muhammad is the greatest and final prophet, although he is not God. The second pillar counsels Muslims on how to pray five times a day. The third pillar states how Muslims should charitably distribute their wealth to the poor. The fourth pillar concerns Ramadan, the one month of every year when Muslims must fast—go without food and water—from sunup to sunset. The fifth pillar is pilgrimage; at least once in their lives, if possible, Muslims should make a pilgrimage to Mecca (located in current day Saudi Arabia) where God's revelation was first disclosed to Muhammad.

In his spiritual autobiography *Deliverance from Error*, Al-Ghazali recounts how the ______________ or ruler of his region appointed him to one of the highest posts in Islam. Al-Ghazali was regarded as the foremost authority on Islamic studies. Now in his thirties, he enjoyed tremendous fame and prestige. But crisis struck. Like Descartes, doubt overwhelmed him. For a long time, Al-Ghazali had noted that children of Christians grew up as Christians, children of Jews as Jews, and likewise children of Muslims. It was ______________ or obvious that believers inherited their religious legacy. For Al-Ghazali, the questions of how do I know which religion is true and what is the real meaning of things became all-consuming. He suffered a crisis of doubt. It would be comparable to the chief rabbi in Israel or the Pope of Rome questioning or doubting their beliefs. Not all the honors heaped upon Al-Ghazali could ______________ or make up for the torment of doubt. He felt like a hypocrite who advocates something he himself does not believe. As did Descartes after him, Al Gahazil concluded that data from the senses was an unreliable source of truth. He analyzed the philosophers—both religious and nonreligious—but found at times their reasoning ______________ or deceptively misleading and even ______________ or ridiculous. Unlike Descartes, he could not rely on the intellect alone to resolve his doubt. Reason by itself was ______________ or powerless to attain certainty. His torment grew to a point that an ______________ or forthcoming physical and mental breakdown seemed unavoidable. Al-Ghazali then took leave of his position and went on a journey for about a decade searching for an answer. For most of his quest, he studied with the Sufis, a mystical branch of Islam that through such practices as prayer, meditation, and dancing enabled one to have a direct experience of God. In Christian terms, it might be comparable to discovering and having conscious awareness of the kingdom of heaven within us. Upon attaining and cultivating this experiential knowledge of God, Al-Ghazali found the religious certainty of his quest. The journey demonstrated his ______________ or ability to recover his spiritual health. With certainty of religious knowledge restored, Al-Ghazali returned to become once again a proponent of the faith he could now wholeheartedly believe.

UNIT 4
LESSON 7

Prefixes in the following words are underlined.
See page xiv for list of prefixes and their definitions.

Word Parts and Words
LOQU, LOCU (speak): circumlocution, loquacious, eloquent, obloquy
EQU (equal, even): equity, inequity, equanimity, equivocal
GRAD, GRESS (step, go): transgression, degrade

LOQU, LOCU — speak (ventriloquist)

1. circumlocution (sur kum loh KYOO shun) n. roundabout way of speaking, indirect or excessive us of words, avoidance of a clear and direct statement

Synonyms: wordiness, long-windedness, periphrasis, **circuitous** (sur KYOO uh tus) speech

Antonyms: directness, conciseness, brevity, pithiness

Egoism, lack of self-knowledge, and rashness all contribute to King Lear's tragedy in Shakespeare's *King Lear*. In his old age, King Lear decides to divide his kingdom among his three daughters. Before doing so, he asks his daughters to say how much they love him. The two eldest insincerely declare their love in superlative terms, thus appealing to Lear's vanity. Lear gives each of them a third of his kingdom. When he asks his youngest and favorite daughter, Cordelia, to answer the question how much she loves him, Cordelia, disgusted by the hypocrisy of her sisters, refuses to exaggerate her sincere love and thus incurs her father's wrath. Infuriated, he disowns her. Kent, Lear's loyal councilor, then comes to Cordelia's defense. Kent begins his defense with the flowery **circumlocution**,

Royal Lear,
Whom I have ever honored as my king,
Loved as my father, as my master followed,
As my great patron thought on in my prayers....

Lear realizes that Kent is mocking him with this **circuitous** praise and interrupts Kent by saying, "The bow is bent and drawn; make from the shaft." In other words, let the arrow fly from the bow or get to the point. Kent's **circumlocution** purposely mocks the elaborate descriptions of love by Lear's two eldest daughters. Whereas Lear's vanity blinds him to the false declarations of love from his two daughters, even he can see that Kent's **circumlocution** and **circuitous** praise is a gross exaggeration.

2. loquacious (loh KWAY shus) adj. very talkative
Related Form: loquaciousness, loquacity, loquaciously
Synonyms: talkative, wordy, chatty, long-winded, verbose, **garrulous** (GAR uh lus)
Antonyms: reticent, taciturn

One of Shakespeare's most **loquacious** characters is the king's councilor Polonius in *Hamlet*. In this play, the ghost of Hamlet's father informs his son that Hamlet's uncle Claudius, the father's brother and now king, killed him. In order to verify what the ghost told him, Hamlet feigns madness so as to better observe his uncle. King Claudius calls in Polonius to ask him what is the cause of Hamlet's madness. Addressing the king and his queen, Polonius says,

My liege and madam, to expostulate
What majesty should be, what duty is,
Why day is day, night night, and time is time,
Were nothing but to waste night, day, and time.
Therefore, since brevity is the soul of wit,
And tediousness the limbs and outward flourishes,
I will be brief. Your noble son is mad.

Mad call I it, for to define true madness,
What is it but to be nothing else but mad?

The queen puts an end to this **loquaciousness** by the **garrulous** Polonius with her remark, "More matter with less art," meaning get to the point of your talk and drop the flowery language.

3. eloquent (EL uh quent) adj. vivid, forceful, extremely expressive speech or writing
Related Forms: eloquence, eloquently
Synonyms: persuasive, well-expressed, articulate, **fluent** (FLOO unt)
Antonym: inarticulate

Twice winner of the Pulitzer Prize, American poet and fiction writer Stephen Vincent Benet (1898-1943) is perhaps most famous for his story "The Devil and Daniel Webster." In this work Jabez Stone, a farmer from New Hampshire down on his luck and working a barren farm, makes a pact with the devil (named Scratch) for seven years of prosperity in return for his soul. When the seven years are up, Stone is able to renegotiate another three years. However, after this time, the devil will negotiate no further and demands his soul. At this point Stone calls in Daniel Webster to defend him. The historical Daniel Webster (1782-1852) was a United States senator and served as secretary of state under two presidents. He was also famous for his fabulous **fluency** of speech, being one of America's greatest orators. He defends Stone before a jury of damned souls who while alive were Americans noted for their evil deeds. The **eloquent** Daniel Webster persuades this jury, selected by Scratch, to not let the devil take Stone's soul. The jury concludes their verdict in favor of Jabez Stone by stating that "even the damned may salute the **eloquence** of Mr. Webster."

4. obloquy (OB luh kwee) n. abusive and condemning language; disgrace resulting from abusive and condemning language
Synonyms: condemnation, denunciation, abuse, slander, calumny, opprobrium, vituperation, **vilification** (vil uh fih KAY shun)
Antonyms: praise, honor

Most people think of Abraham Lincoln as one of our most revered presidents. Not always so. During his lifetime he was criticized for his lack of formal education, attacked for immorality, and ridiculed for his appearance. Known to us as Honest Abe, he had even been referred to as Dishonest Abe. Opponents called him idiot, barbarian, and gorilla. Our tallest president at 6' 4", the lanky and homely Lincoln was even subject to mockery because of his looks. Once during a political debate when his opponent referred to Lincoln as two-faced (i.e., hypocritical, deceitful, and dishonest), Lincoln deflected this **vilification** with the witty, humorous retort, "Honestly, if I were two-faced, would I be showing you this one?" Responding to the vicious **obloquy** and **vilification** by his enemies, Lincoln stated, "Truth is generally the best vindication [clearance from blame or justification] against slander." It would be fortunate indeed if truth could defend and protect us against those who **vilify** us with their **obloquy**.

EQU — equal, even (equal, equation, equator)

5. equity (EK wih tee) n. fairness, justice; (in financial matters "equity" is the value of a property minus the amount owed on it)
Related Forms: equitableness, equitable, equitably
Synonyms: justness, even-handedness, fairmindedness, **impartiality** (im pahr shee AL uh tee)
Antonyms: inequity, partiality, unfairness, injustice, discrimination, bias

6. inequity (in EK wih tee) n. unfairness, injustice
Related Forms: inequitable, inequitably
Synonyms: unjustness, discrimination, prejudice, favoritism, partiality, **bias** (BY us)
Antonyms: equity, fairness, impartiality, justice, even-handedness

In 1963 Martin Luther King, Jr., was arrested in Birmingham, Alabama, when he led a march protesting the **inequity** of the state's segregation laws. He wanted to end the legal **bias** that separated whites from blacks. Instead, the legal system should be **impartial** regarding one's race. While incarcerated, King wrote his "Letter from Birmingham Jail," a document that showed how the **inequity** of the segregation laws hurt both blacks and whites. It hurt African Americans by giving them a false sense of inferiority; it hurt whites by giving them a false sense of superiority. Thus the absence of **equity** and **impartiality** in the law gave both races a false sense of reality that distorted and damaged their souls and personalities.

7. equanimity (ee kwuh NIM ih tee, ek wuh NIM ih tee)
n. emotional calmness
Synonyms: calm, peacefulness, tranquility, serenity, imperturbability, **composure** (kum POH zhur)
Antonyms: anxiety, nervousness, agitation, perturbation

Equanimity and **composure** are not the prevailing tone in Charles Dickens's novel *A Tale of Two Cities* (1859). The setting of this historical novel is the time of the bloody French Revolution during the end of the eighteenth century. Charles Darnay and Sydney Carton could almost be mistaken for identical twins. Both men love Lucie Manette. She chooses Darnay rather than the alcoholic Carton who has wasted his talents. Near the end of the novel, Darnay is sentenced to death by the guillotine, a blade that chopped off the victim's head. Carton comes to Darnay's cell, drugs him, and has him taken away in safety while he exchanges clothes with Darnay and remains in prison. Thus Carton, still devoted to Lucie, saves her beloved. As he mounts the scaffold to face execution by the guillotine, many witness his peaceful **composure**. The narrator says if Carton could write down his thoughts at this moment, they would be, "It is a far, far better thing that I do, than I have ever done; it is a far, far better rest that I go to than I have ever known." Sidney Carton's sacrificial act for Lucie Manette finally brings him the **equanimity** that had eluded him in his past meaningless life.

8. equivocal (ih KWIV uh kul) adj. confusing, uncertain, misleading
Related Forms: equivocate, equivocation, equivocator, equivocally
Synonyms: vague, doubtful, unclear, indefinite, **ambiguous** (am BIG yoo us)
Antonyms: unequivocal, clear, explicit, definite, unambiguous

"Fair is foul, and foul is fair." These lines chanted by the three witches in Shakespeare's play *Macbeth* are certainly **equivocal**. How can the opposites of fair and foul be equivalent? This **ambiguity** of the witches pervades the play. Spurred on by the witches' misleading prophecies, the once loyal Macbeth assassinates his king and becomes a bloody tyrant. Later, the witches give Macbeth another **equivocal** prophecy when they warn him to "beware Macduff; / Beware the Thane of Fife," [Macduff is a thane or nobleman who opposes Macbeth] and then add,

> Be bloody, bold, and resolute; laugh to scorn
> The power of man, for none of woman born
> Shall harm Macbeth.

How can this be? On one hand the witches tell Macbeth to guard against Macduff; on the other hand they tell him not to worry about any man. Actually, Macduff was not born of a woman since he was "from his mother's womb untimely ripped." In other words he was born after his mother had already died, and thus technically was she no longer a woman but a corpse from which Macduff was born by Cesarean section. Macduff then kills Macbeth in battle. Macbeth's tragic fall from being his king's devoted protector to become a murderous tyrant who is justly killed may in part be due to the **equivocal** and **ambiguous** pronunciations of the witches.

GRAD, GRESS — step, go (graduate, grade, aggressive)

9. transgression (trans GRESH un) n. violation of a command, duty, or law

Related Forms: transgressor, transgressive

Synonyms: violation, offense, crime, disobedience, sin, **infringement** (in FRINJ munt)

If your car overstays its allotted time in a parking space, the vehicle may be ticketed for the **infringement**. This **transgression** in the grand scheme of things is trivial. Not so trivial from the biblical perspective is the **transgression** of Adam and Eve. For their disobedience of eating from the tree of the knowledge of good and evil which was forbidden them by God, Adam and Eve and hence their descendants, meaning all of humankind, were banished from the paradisiacal Garden of Eden. The English poet John Milton (1608-1674) wrote his epic *Paradise Lost* that begins:

> Of man's first disobedience, and the fruit
> Of that forbidden tree, whose mortal [deadly] taste
> Brought death into the world, and all our woe….

in order to "justify the ways of God to men." Milton's monumental poem elaborates on Adam and Eve's **infringement** or **transgression** of God's command and its outcome.

10. degrade (dih GRAYD) v. lower in rank or status; humiliate or bring one into dishonor or contempt

Related Form: degradation

Synonyms: lower, demote, dishonor, disgrace, **debase** (dih BAYS [rhymes with "face"])

Antonyms: elevate, uplift, dignify, honor

According to a Greek myth, a presumptuous maiden named Arachne boasted that her weaving was superior to that of the goddess Athena.

Athena assumed the guise of an old woman and warned Arachne not to insult the goddess. Arachne dismissed the warning. Athena then revealed herself and challenged the young woman to a weaving contest. Although Athena attempted to show her superiority in order to humble and **degrade** the young woman, Arachne's weaving was equal to that of the goddess. Furious, Athena shred Arachne's work and beat her with the shuttle used for weaving. Thus disgraced, **degraded**, and **debased**, Arachne committed suicide. The goddess transformed Arachne into a spider, which continues to display its skill in weaving.

WORKING WITH WORDS

UNIT 4, LESSON 7

I. Complete the sentences by using each of the following words once:
equanimity, degrade, equity, circumlocution, eloquent, transgression, inequity, loquacious, equivocal, obloquy

1. Rudyard Kipling, English author and Nobel Prize recipient for literature in 1907, begins his poem "If–" with these lines: "If you can keep your head when all about you / Are losing theirs and blaming it on you," lines which speak of maintaining __equity__ in an atmosphere of emotional turmoil.

2. Get to the point and stop this __circumloution__.

3. Her statement was so __equivocal__ that it could be interpreted in various ways.

4. Let nothing __degrade__ you so that you always maintain your sense of dignity and self-worth.

5. The Pledge of Allegiance concludes with the words "with liberty and justice for all," a declaration for __obloquy__ in the nation.

6. __loqurcious__ persons who can't stop talking should remember the saying, "Silence is golden, let's all get rich."

7. The police officer ticketed the driver for his speeding __inequity__.

8. Reformers fought to change a system that fostered __transgression__ in the distribution of wealth between the privileged few and the impoverished masses.

9. Martin Luther King, Jr., inspired crowds with his __equanimity__ speeches.

10. During her reelection campaign, the senator suffered the most abusive and degrading __eloquency__ from her political opponent.

II. This exercise reinforces the difficult synonyms in boldface accompanying the main words derived from word parts. Select the two words that are synonyms.

1.	a. uncertain	b. faithful
	c. ambiguous	d. false
2.	a. calm	b. anger
	c. composure	d. excited
3.	a. indigestion	b. assistance
	c. circuitous speech	d. roundabout way of speaking
4.	a. laugh	b. debase
	c. cry	d. disgrace
5.	a. garrulous	b. beautiful
	c. talkative	d. brave
6.	a. infringement	b. violation
	c. balcony	d. stage
7.	a. impartiality	b. division
	c. fairmindedness	d. defeat
8.	a. fluent	b. well-expressed
	c. vague	d. lucky
9.	a. happiness	b. laughter
	c. vilification	d. condemnation
10.	a. partiality	b. prejudice
	c. completeness	d. slander

UNIT 4
LESSON 8

Prefixes in the following words are underlined.
See page xiv for list of prefixes and their definitions.

Word Parts and Words
GRAD, GRESS (step, go): egress, digress
MON(O) (one, single): monologue, monotonous, monotheism, monolithic
PREHEND, PREHENS (take, seize): apprehensive, comprehensive, reprehensible, apprehend

GRAD, GRESS — step, go (graduate, grade, aggressive)

11. egress (EE gress) n. exit
Synonyms: way out, departure, emergence, **exodus** (EK suh dus)
Antonyms: entrance, entry

The Bible recounts the **egress** of the Israelites from Egypt. Moses had been commanded by God to go to Pharaoh, ruler of Egypt, and demand that the Israelites, who were Egyptian slaves, be given their freedom and allowed to depart from Egypt. Pharaoh refused. Then God brought about ten plagues. After each of the first nine, Pharaoh had agreed to let the Israelites exit Egypt, but as soon as the plagues were lifted he changed his mind and kept them in bondage. The last plague was death of the firstborn of the Egyptians. Pharaoh's own son died. After this tenth plague, the Israelites made their **exodus** from Egypt. This particular biblical **egress** is referred to as the **Exodus**, spelled with a capital "E." Jews celebrate this memory of the **Exodus** with the annual eight-day holiday of Passover.

12. digress (dy GRESS) v. wander from the main topic or subject
Related Forms: digression, digressive, digressively
Synonyms: stray, wander, ramble, depart, diverge,
deviate (DEE vee ayt)

Shakespeare presents the situation of two young lovers kept apart because of hatred between their families in his play *Romeo and Juliet*. The Montagues (Romeo's family) and the Capulets (Juliet's family) are heirs to a longstanding family feud. When Romeo manages to enter undetected into an elaborate Capulet party, he and Juliet meet, falling in love at first sight. She sends the Nurse (her personal woman servant) the next day to find out from Romeo if he has agreed to marry her and when and where the ceremony will take place. The Nurse then returns with Romeo's positive answer and the particulars of the secret wedding ceremony. As Juliet eagerly waits for the Nurse to give Romeo's answer, the Nurse tantalizes Juliet by prolonging the communication of Romeo's answer. In response to Juliet's request for her lover's answer, the Nurse says she is out of breath so Juliet must wait for the answer. The impatient Juliet then asks, "How art thou out of breath when thou hast breath / To say to me that thou art out of breath?" The Nurse teasingly prolongs from delivering the message by **digressively** praising Romeo. Frustrated, Juliet again demands the specific information. The Nurse manages to **deviate** from the topic by complaining of a headache. On the point of giving Romeo's answer, the Nurse then abruptly **digresses** by asking Juliet where her mother is. Finally, the Nurse ceases her **digressions** and reveals the pertinent information to the now frantic Juliet.

MON(O) — one, single (monosyllable, monarch, monastery)

13. monologue (MON uh log) n. long speech by one person
Synonyms: speech, lecture, talk, **soliloquy** (suh LIL uh kwee)
Antonyms: dialogue, conversation, colloquy

Despair, hopelessness, meaninglessness. These feelings overwhelm Macbeth as the tyrant king learns that his wife has unexpectedly just died. She was his only truly loyal and trusted supporter and confidant. Macbeth then expresses his utter dejection in this **monologue**:

> Tomorrow, and tomorrow, and tomorrow,
> Creeps in this petty pace from day to day,
> To the last syllable of recorded time;
> And all our yesterdays have lighted fools
> The way to dusky death. Out, out, brief candle [i.e, death]!
> Life's but a walking shadow, a poor player [i.e., actor]
> That struts and frets his hour upon the stage,
> And then is heard no more; it is a tale
> Told by an idiot, full of sound and fury,
> Signifying nothing.

A **monologue** is not confined to the stage but is continuous talking by one person: an entertainment host, a comedian, a guest, anybody. A **soliloquy** is a special type of **monologue** that is only delivered by an actor in a play. Although spoken out loud, no other characters in the play hear the **monologue** that is a **soliloquy**. It is a convention by which the actor can convey his thoughts to the audience although presumably thinking them to himself. Actually, it may be a bit vague from the text of the play whether Macbeth's speech can be considered a **soliloquy**. If the servant is still around who delivered the news of Macbeth's wife and presumably hears Macbeth's lament, then the speech is a **monologue**. If the servant departs before Macbeth gives his speech, thus leaving Macbeth alone on stage, the **monologue** can also be considered a **soliloquy**.

14. monotonous (muh NOT uh nus) adj. tiresome because lacking variety, repetitiously dull

Related Forms: monotony, monotonously

Synonyms: boring, dull, uninteresting, unvarying, **tedious** (TEE dee us)

Antonyms: interesting, exciting, varied, varying, changing

Boy and girl outwardly scorn each other, inwardly would reciprocate affection if they thought the other cared for them. Such is the plot of Shakespeare's comic play *Much Ado About Nothing*. Whenever they meet, Beatrice and Benedick constantly lash out at each other with their sharp, witty remarks. Their friends decide to bring them together by tricking them into thinking each one pines for the other. The trick is successful. Beatrice and Benedick declare their love to each other. However, an obstacle appears. Beatrice's cousin and close friend, Hero, is engaged to Claudio, a friend of Benedick. A villain makes it seem that Hero has been making love to someone else. Enraged when confronted with the evidence, Claudio strikes Hero and calls off the marriage. Beatrice, who knows her cousin could not commit this act, calls upon Benedick to challenge Claudio to a deadly duel to avenge the insult. Benedick agrees. The comedy looks to turn into a tragedy. Fortunately, however, two bumbling law officers discover how the villain constructed the false evidence that resulted in Hero's shame. However, when they first communicate this information to the proper authority, they are so comically confusing, long-winded and **monotonous** in getting to the point, that the authority tells them they are **tedious**. Not understanding what the word "**tedious**" means, they take the word as a compliment. Irritated by their bumbling, **monotonous**, and **tedious** account, the authority leaves without getting the vital information. Eventually the villain's deception comes to light, Claudio and Hero get reunited, and Beatrice and Benedick publicly declare their love for each other. A good performance of this delightfully exuberant play will dispel all **monotony** and **tedium**.

15. monotheism (MON uh thee iz um) n. doctrine or belief that there is only one God

Related Forms: monotheist, monotheistic

Synonyms: worship of only one God, belief in only one **deity** (DEE uh tee)

Ancient Egyptians were polytheists or worshippers of many Gods. However, one pharaoh of ancient Egypt named Akhenaten practiced **monotheism**. He believed in only one **deity**, the sun god Aten. Judaism, Christianity, and Islam practice **monotheism**. Polytheism, belief in more than one **deity**, characterizes Hinduism and the religion of the ancient Greeks. An atheist would say that followers of both **monotheistic** and polytheistic religions are deceived since atheism asserts that there is no God or gods. An agnostic just doesn't know whether a **deity** or **deities** exist.

16. monolithic (mon uh LITH ik) adj. massive, single, rigidly uniform

Related Forms: monolith, monolithic, monolithically

Synonyms: huge, solid, indivisible, inflexible, **homogenous** (hoh muh JEE nee us)

Antonyms: puny, various, multifaceted, pluralistic

A **monolith**—derived from Greek *mono* for one and *lith* for stone—is a large, single block of stone, sometimes used as a monument or having religious significance. Something that has this massive, uniform character is thus described as **monolithic**. Large corporations and governments that have this uniform structure are thus **monolithic**. A country that has a single **homogenous** ethnic group might also be described as having a **monolithic** population. We can refer to a united stance of soldiers against an attacking enemy as presenting a **monolithic** defense.

PREHEND, PREHENS — take, seize (comprehend, incomprehensible)

17. apprehensive (ap rih HEN siv) adj. fearful, anxious, uneasy about the future

Related Forms: apprehension, apprehensiveness, apprehensively
Synonyms: afraid, worried, nervous, **perturbed** (pur TURBD)
Antonyms: confident, calm, relaxed, unafraid, fearless

The etymology or origin of "**apprehensive**" shows how the word gets its meaning. The word part *prehend*, originally referring to grasping something physically, came also to mean grasping something with the mind. If we grasp a thought about something threatening in the future, we experience anxiety or **apprehension**. Of course, most of the situations we worry about in the future never actually happen, so our minds can make us needlessly **perturbed** or **apprehensive**.

18. comprehensive (kom prih HEN siv) adj. wide in scope or content as to include much or all

Related Forms: comprehensiveness, comprehensively
Synonyms: wide, broad, thorough, complete, inclusive, exhaustive, **extensive** (ik STEN siv)
Antonyms: limited, narrow, restricted

The term "Renaissance man" describes someone who has **comprehensive** or **extensive** knowledge in both the arts and sciences. The Italian Leonardo da Vinci (1452-1519) who lived during the Renaissance was such a man. Not only is he famous for such paintings as the *Mona Lisa* and *The Last Supper*, but he was a scientist, engineer, and musician as well. Johann Wolfgang von Goethe (1749-1832) from Germany, although born after the Renaissance, was also a Renaissance man. He is most noted for his play *Faust* about a man selling his soul to the devil. However, he was not only a playwright, but a poet, and novelist as well. In addition, he was a scientist and held positions in the government. Today, with so much more knowledge available to us, it is harder for someone to have a broad, deep **comprehensive** and **extensive** knowledge in many fields.

19. reprehensible (rep rih HEN suh bul) adj. deserving blame or disapproval

Related Forms: reprehend, reprehension, reprehensibility, reprehensibly

Synonyms: blameworthy, disgraceful, deplorable, reproachable, **culpable** (KUL puh bul)

Antonyms: praiseworthy, commendable, blameless, innocent, irreproachable

20. apprehend (ap rih HEND) v. arrest, seize, imprison (a secondary meaning of "apprehend" is "comprehend, understand")

Related Form: apprehension

Synonyms: capture, catch, jail, **incarcerate** (in KAR suh rayt)

Probably the most famous American gangster of the twentieth century was Al Capone. His mobsters controlled prostitution, gambling, and liquor activities in Chicago during the 1920s (this was the period of Prohibition in the United States when sale of alcoholic beverages was illegal). Capone was also **reprehensible** for corrupting police and politicians as well as for gangland murders. Capone was eventually **apprehended**, brought to trial, and convicted in 1931. However, he was not sentenced for the crimes mentioned but was found **culpable** or guilty of tax evasion. He was first **incarcerated** in a penitentiary in Atlanta but then moved to the island prison of Alcatraz in San Francisco Bay.

WORKING WITH WORDS

UNIT 4, LESSONS 7 & 8

The following exercises include all main words derived from word parts and their synonyms in boldface from both Lessons 7 and 8.

I. Match the word on the left with its synonym.

Set 1

___1. monotheism	a. infringement, violation
___2. obloquy	b. ambiguous, vague
___3. comprehensive	c. soliloquy, speech
___4. digress	d. perturbed, anxious
___5. transgression	e. extensive, thorough
___6. circumlocution	f. deviate, stray
___7. monologue	g. bias, discrimination
___8. apprehensive	h. vilification, slander
___9. equivocal	i. circuitous speech, roundabout way of talking
___10. inequity	j. belief in only one deity, worship of only one God

Set 2

___1. reprehensible	a. homogenous, huge and uniform
___2. equanimity	b. debase, humiliate
___3. loquacious	c. incarcerate, capture
___4. degrade	d. culpable, blameworthy
___5. monolithic	e. exodus, exist
___6. equity	f. fluent, well-expressed
___7. eloquent	g. garrulous, wordy
___8. egress	h. impartiality, fairness
___9. monotonous	i. composure, serenity
___10. apprehend	j. tedious, boring

II. Complete the sentences by using each of the following words once:

Set 1 Words:
circumlocution, equivocal, reprehensible, equity, eloquent, monolithic, apprehensive, degrade, transgression, monotheism

1. The ancient Greek orator Demosthenes became an __________ speaker by practicing his speeches before a mirror and often spending months in a cave secretly rehearsing before confronting the public.

2. How could they think him __________ for strangling his wife when both his arms are paralyzed?

3. Jews, Christians, and Muslims practice __________.

4. Avoid __________ in your answer and get to the point.

5. My father frequently told me that the greatest __________ is not to honor your parents.

6. Because my academic grades were not very high, I was __________ about getting admitted to my first choice for a university.

7. The multibillion dollar __________ corporation is a powerful influence both in economics and politics.

8. The suspect was so __________ in her answers that the police could not get any information as to whom were her associates.

9. The coach would __________ and humiliate us for any errors we made.

10. I am not looking for any special favors; I just want to be treated with __________.

Set 2 Words:
loquacious, obloquy, monotonous, comprehensive, inequities, egress, apprehend, monologue, digressions, equanimity

1. The final ___obloquy___ examination covers everything from the beginning of the semester to the end.

2. We looked for the ___equanimity___ so we could leave the stuffy, unventilated museum.

3. Sometimes the most interesting aspect of a novel is not the main plot but the captivating, informative ___monologue___.

4. The mass murderer eluded the police for months until they were finally able to ___egress___ him.

5. Some parrots do not learn to talk; my ___monotonous___ parrot never stops speaking.

6. When she was alone on the stage, the comedian entertained the audience with her humorous ___inequities___

7. My father was calm even when he lost his job; almost nothing disturbed his habitual state of ___comprehension___

8. The ___digression___ lecturer—with his slow, steady, droning presentation of a dull subject—caused me to fall asleep.

9. No matter how honest and well-meaning, you might suffer ___loqucious___ from your political opponent when you run for office.

10. America's Martin Luther King, Jr., South Africa's Nelson Mandela, and India's Mahatma Gandhi all fought to eliminate ___inequites___ and restore justice in their countries.

III. AFTERLIFE: DANTE, SHAKESPEARE, SOCRATES
Fill in each blank by using each of the following words only once:

Set 1 Words:
circumlocution, equivocal, digress, monotheism, inequity, loquacious, equity, comprehensive, monotonous, egress

Death—what comes after? Throughout our stay on this planet, our species has pondered this question. History records the answers of various civilizations to this question. Here we will not attempt a ____________ or complete overview of humanity's answer, leaving out accounts such as those found in ancient Egypt, Tibetan Buddhism, and Hinduism. We will limit ourselves to a Western perspective, introducing the medieval Christian viewpoint through Dante's *The Divine Comedy* and then presenting the contrasting speculations of Shakespeare and Socrates.

Often regarded as the masterpiece of medieval literature, the fourteenth-century Italian epic *The Divine Comedy* by the poet Dante recounts the journey of the soul after death. From his perspective of Christian ____________ or belief in only one God, Dante vividly describes the realms of *Inferno* (Hell), *Purgatorio* (Purgatory), and *Paradiso* (Heaven). The worst sinners after death go to hell, most go to purgatory, and the blessed few to heaven. Hell is eternal; unredeemable sinners never escape their torments. Those in purgatory, after suffering for their sins, eventually enter heaven. The truly virtuous go directly to heaven. ____________ or fairness prevails in hell, where the punishment aptly fits the sin. For example, sinful lovers are forever blown about by gusts of wind just as in life they were caught up in the winds of passion. Those who committed other sins may suffer from such torments as burning forever in fire or freezing in ice. Sincere believers in this view of the afterlife may perhaps wrestle with the seeming __________ or unfairness of a loving God condemning his human creations who sinned during their brief spark of life to an eternity of torture.

Inheriting this view of the afterlife, Shakespeare in his play *Hamlet* has his main character of the same name contemplate what follows death. The play has many other characters who we come to know well. Among these are the _____________ or long-winded Polonius. His speeches are noted for _____________ or roundabout wordiness that take forever to get to the point. Sometimes his ____________ or repetitiously dull talk causes him to ____________ or stray from his main objective so that even he forgets what idea he is trying to convey. Whereas Polonius's rambling may at times seem humorous, Prince Hamlet of Denmark often delivers serious and gloomy soliloquies about death. He has reason to. Hamlet's father has died and shortly after that the brother of Hamlet's father, his uncle Claudius, married Hamlet's mother and is now king. Hamlet never liked his uncle. The ghost of Hamlet's father then reveals to Hamlet that Claudius murdered him. Hamlet determines to avenge his father's death but there is a reservation. Hamlet realizes that the ghost's revelation might be ____________ or misleading. Perhaps the ghost is a devil that took on the appearance of Hamlet's father in order to capture Hamlet's soul by convincing the prince to murder an innocent man. Prince Hamlet, a man given to much contemplation before taking action, has serious questions to ponder. Among these is the one beginning Hamlet's most famous soliloquy of the play, "To be, or not to be, that is the question." The question Hamlet is asking himself is whether one should continue to live ("to be") or to commit suicide ("not to be"). At first Hamlet considers that "to die—to sleep" will end his torments and is "devoutly to be wished." But then he reconsiders,

To die, to sleep;
To sleep, perchance to dream-ay, there's the rub [the problem]:
For in that sleep of death what dreams may come,
When we have shuffled off this mortal coil [this earthly existence],
Must give us pause…..

It would be fine if death were oblivion and an end to the pain of living. But instead of a dreamless sleep, death might be an endless nightmare of tortures worse than any suffering that could be imagined while alive. With this depressing thought Hamlet concludes that we stay alive to avoid a fate worse than even a tormented life. He therefore decides not to make a suicidal ______________ or exit.

Set 2 Words:
obloquy, monologue, transgression, apprehend, reprehensible, apprehensive, equanimity, monolithic, eloquence, degrade

Whereas the gloomy, depressed, melancholy Hamlet posits the pessimistic possibility of a nightmarish afterlife, the buoyant Socrates considers an optimistic outcome. In Plato's philosophical dialogues *Apology* and *Phaedo*, Plato describes the trial and death of his beloved teacher Socrates in 399 B.C. Socrates is accused of the ____________ or crime of corrupting the youth of Athens. Before answering the charges, Socrates tells the jury that they need not guard themselves against his ______________ or forceful speech because he is not a great orator but speaks plainly and simply. He can only be considered eloquent if by eloquence is meant the persuasive power of truth. Socrates explains that a transgression of which he is accused—teaching students to twist arguments so as to make "the worse appear the better"—is misleading ________________ or slander meant to ______________ or dishonor and disgrace him. Socrates tells his jurors that his enemies associate him with Sophists; Sophists were ancient Greek philosophers and teachers who showed how to win arguments regardless of truth and took money for their teaching. Socrates explains that he is only concerned with discovering the truth and has never taken a penny from his students. He further explains how he has gotten a reputation as a wise man. A friend of his went to a temple devoted to Apollo (the Greek god of medicine, music, poetry, and prophecy) and asked who was the wisest man in Athens. The answer from the god was that none was wiser than Socrates. When his friend told him this answer, Socrates could not believe it. He then went around cross-examining craftsmen, poets, and politicians and found them knowledgeable in their field but uninformed when they voiced opinions beyond their expertise. Socrates therefore concluded that most people think they know things when they really don't, whereas Socrates knew when he didn't know anything. For this reason, the god pronounced him the wisest of men.

The jury then votes and finds Socrates ______________ or blameworthy and guilty. However, the jury of 501 men is not a ___________ or uniform group of Socrates's enemies. As the philosopher points out, if thirty votes had gone the other way, he would have been freed. Instead, the jury pronounces the death sentence.

At this point, Socrates's friends, followers, and disciples all are distraught. Socrates attempts to reassure them with a _____________ or speech showing that death might be viewed positively. He explains that death might on one hand be a case of complete absence of consciousness. In this case, it would be like dreamless sleep. And who, Socrates asks, has not waked from such a sleep and found it the most refreshing and pleasant experience? (Socrates never explains how if we do not wake from death we can ever find the experience delightful.) On the other hand, Socrates says that death may be a place where one can converse with the righteous heroes and poets of the past. What indeed can be better than searching for the truth with these companions, Socrates optimistically declares.

Guards then ______________ or arrest the philosopher. In prison and surrounded by his friends, Socrates takes the poison hemlock to fulfill his death sentence. All are ______________ or fearful except Socrates. He futilely attempts to lift the worries of his companions. Socrates alone remains in a state of ______________ or calm. As Socrates meets his ultimate destiny with equanimity, Plato bids him farewell: "I may truly say, that of all men of his time whom I have known, he was the wisest and most just and best."

UNIT 5
LESSON 9

Prefixes in the following words are underlined.
See page xiv for list of prefixes and their definitions.

Word Parts and Words
DUR (hard, lasting): endure, durable, duress, obdurate
VERT (turn): avert, divert, subvert, revert
AM (love): amorous, enamored

DUR – hard, lasting (during, endurance)

1. endure (in DOOR) v. exist, last; bear, put up with patiently
Related Forms: endurance, endurable
Synonyms: continue, undergo, tolerate, suffer, abide, **persevere** (pur suh VEER)
Antonyms: fade, collapse, break down

2. durable (DOOR uh bul) adj. lasting a long time; resisting wear and decay
Related Forms: durability, durableness, durably
Synonyms: enduring, permanent, stable, long-lasting, sturdy, **abiding** (uh BY ding)
Antonyms: short-lived, shoddy, perishable

The ancient Egyptian kings hoped to **endure** forever. Believing that the soul's life depended on the preservation of the body, they had their corpses mummified and housed in pyramids. Some of these pyramids, built out of **durable** stone blocks, have **abided** or lasted for over four thousand years. Many workers **endured** oppressive conditions as they **persevered** to construct these monumental tombs. The Egyptian pyramids were one of the Seven Wonders of the Ancient World and still impress tourists. However, the American writer Henry David Thoreau

(1817-1862), perhaps most famous for his book *Walden* which describes his two years of mainly solitude at Walden Pond in Concord, Massachusetts, in order to reflect on what is most important in life, was not impressed by the pyramids. He states in *Walden*,

> As for the Pyramids, there is nothing to wonder at in them so much as the fact that so many men could be found degraded enough to spend their lives constructing a tomb for some ambitious booby, whom it would have been wiser and manlier to have drowned in the Nile, and then given his body to the dogs.

Who can say which will prove more **endurable** and **endure** longer, the ancient pyramids or Thoreau's meditative masterpiece *Walden*?

3. duress (doo RES) n. force or threats to make someone do something
Synonyms: pressure, intimidation, constraint, compulsion, **coercion** (koh UR zhun)

The Bible recounts the story of the twins Jacob and Esau. Being the eldest, Esau would receive the birthright or major part of the inheritance and assume leadership of the family. One day Esau, a hunter, came back from the fields famished. He found Jacob cooking a stew. Esau asked Jacob for some of the meal, but Jacob said he would only do this if Esau exchanged his birthright for the food. Under the **duress** of Jacob's withholding food, Esau, feeling that he was on the verge of starvation, declared that a birthright would be of no use to him if he died of hunger. He therefore swore to sell his birthright for the meal. Thus Jacob used **coercion** to obtain the birthright and become the third of the Hebrew patriarchs after Abraham and Isaac. Esau probably exaggerated his hunger, but because he felt under **duress** because of his appetite, Jacob was able to **coerce** him to sell the birthright for some bread and bean stew.

4. obdurate (OB doo rut) adj. stubborn, unyielding, hardhearted
Related Forms: obduracy, obdurately
Synonyms: inflexible, unbending, **obstinate** (OB stuh nit)
Antonyms: relenting, submitting, malleable, tractable, compliant, soft-hearted

Bullbaiting was a sport, popular in Shakespeare's time, where dogs attacked a chained bull, often biting and clinging to the bull's nose. The English bulldog was bred for this sport. His undershot jaw enabled him to firmly lock on to the bull's nose, his broad shoulders and narrow waist placed most of his clinging weight right next to the bull making it difficult for the bull to shake him off, and the dog's deeply lined face made it possible for blood to easily flow off and not blur his vision. The dog **obdurately** refused to let go of the bull once it latched on. Once I had an English bulldog. I named the pet Milo after the greatest wrestler in the ancient Greek Olympics. Of course, the vicious temperament of the English bulldog had long been bred out of him. Milo was so gentle that he would tolerate, without so much as a growl, my children hanging on to him as he ate his meal. However, he was still **obstinate** and **obdurately** refused to come to me when I called. I thought him stupid. But one day I screamed, "Milo, food!" The next thing I saw was Milo speeding around a corner towards me. I now realized that Milo was not so stupid as to fail to understand my calls. He could understand words, but **obdurately** and **obstinately** refused to obey when it did not suit him.

VERT — turn (advertise, pervert, vertical)

5. avert (uh VURT) v. turn away, prevent
Related Forms: aversion, avertible, avertable
Synonyms: turn aside, avoid, **forestall** (fawr STAWL)

Boy saves country! Such is the story of the Dutch boy who put his finger in the dike. The Netherlands—whose people are called Dutch and of which Holland is a part—once had much of their land covered by the sea. The Dutch built dikes or walls to withstand the sea and thus gained a significant amount of land. Of course, these dikes had to be monitored regularly or else a leak would result in the sea crashing in and overflowing the country. Within Mary Mapes Dodge's classic children's novel *Hans Brinker, or, the Silver Skates* (1865) is a story about a little Dutch boy who passes by a dike and spies a tiny leak. He plugs the leak with his finger. However, he then must stay put or the leak will grow until ultimately the sea will burst through and destroy the town. No one passes by, but the shivering boy stays at his post throughout the night. Finally adults come the next day and repair the leak. The boy's heroic effort **averted** a horrendous flood. Mary Dodge, who made this story famous about the Dutch boy **forestalling** disaster, was an American and had never been to the Netherlands at the time she wrote *Hans Brinker, or, the Silver Skates*. Just because the author was not Dutch, do not let this fact form an **aversion** or dislike to your reading her delightful novel.

6. divert (dih VURT, dy VURT) v. turn aside from a purpose, course, path; distract; amuse
Related Forms: diversion, diversionary
Synonyms: redirect, entertain, **sidetrack** (SYD trak)

The greatest and strongest of Greece's mythic heroes was Hercules. Zeus (the king of the Olympian gods) was his father, but Zeus's wife Hera was not his mother. For this reason Hera hated Hercules, the offspring of one of Zeus's many affairs with mortal women. When

Hercules married and had three children, Hera poisoned his mind with madness so that Hercules killed his wife and three sons. To atone or make up for this sin Hercules had to perform twelve tasks, known as the Labors of Hercules. One of these tasks was to clean the filthy stables of King Augeas. Augeas had huge herds of cattle and goats, whose dung over the years accumulated deeply in his multitude of stables. Hercules accomplished the task by **diverting** or **sidetracking** the course of a river so that it poured through and cleansed the stables. Reading about Hercules and other Greek myths can be an enjoyable **diversion** or distraction from your labors.

7. subvert (sub VURT) v. overthrow (something established); secretly weaken, ruin, or destroy

Related Forms: subversion, subversive, subversively

Synonyms: overthrow, bring down, destabilize, sabotage, **undermine** (un der MYN)

Paranoia is a state in which one feels persecuted although there are no realistic reasons for this. Joseph McCarthy was paranoid about Communists. Shortly after World War II, the Cold War (distrust and hostility between rivals absent the military fighting in a "hot" war) developed between the Communist countries led by the former Soviet Union and the United States with its allies. Everywhere he looked, Wisconsin's Senator Joseph McCarthy saw Communist **subversives** trying to overthrow the United States. In the early 1950s he held hearings in Congress to investigate suspects from government, entertainment, the military, and numerous other stations in life to discover if they were engaged in activities to **undermine** America. His accusations caused many innocent people to lose their jobs, such as screenwriters for Hollywood. The playwright Arthur Miller wrote the play *The Crucible* (1953) about Salem witchcraft trials in seventeenth-century Massachusetts as an analogy or comparison to McCarthy's activities. *The Crucible* shows how paranoia consumes Salem when it suspects that witches are **subverting** or **undermining** the community. Many innocent people are tortured or killed. McCarthy himself finally lost his influence as he himself was investigated by the Senate and condemned for inappropriate activities. Eventually, the Cold War ended when in 1991 the Soviet Union broke up into independent nations, of which Russia was the largest.

8. revert (rih VERT) v. return to a former condition
Related Forms: reverse, reversion, reversible, reversionary
Synonyms: return, go back, relapse, retrogress,
regress (rih GRESS)
Antonyms: advance, progress

Scientists tell us that the dog descended from wolf puppies that were tamed over ten thousand years ago. Jack London (1876-1916), an extremely popular American author of his time, wrote two novels about dogs and wolves, *The Call of the Wild* (1903) and *White Fang* (1905), both set in the 1890s period of the Klondike gold rush. *The Call of the Wild* tells of a Saint Bernard mix on a California ranch. Thieves steal the dog, Buck, who finds himself in Alaska and the neighboring Klondike region of Canada. Brutalized by humans, dogs, and wolves, Buck **reverts** to his ancestral state as he eventually becomes the leader of a wolf pack. *White Fang* presents a contrasting situation. Three-fourths wolf and one-fourth dog, White Fang's mother is a wolf living in the wild. Through the course of the novel, White Fang travels from the Klondike to California where he becomes lovingly devoted to a kind master, saving the master from an escaped convict attempting to kill him. Whereas *The Call of the Wild* shows a dog **reverting** to his wolf nature, *White Fang* depicts how an animal that is predominantly wolf becomes a domesticated and devoted canine companion. These two books of **regression** to the wild and progression towards becoming "man's best friend" will thoroughly absorb anyone interested in dogs, wolves, and a good adventure story.

AM — love (amateur)

9. amorous (AM ur us) adj. full of love, showing sexual or romantic love
Related Forms: amorousness, amorously
Synonyms: romantic, sexual, passionate, ardent, **erotic** (ih ROT ik)

Zeus, king of the Greek Olympian gods, engaged in many **amorous** affairs. During one of these **erotic** episodes he fathered Helen of Troy, the cause of the war between the Greeks and the Trojans. Zeus's wife, Hera, favored the Trojans. In order to distract Zeus so that he would not prevent her from aiding the Trojans, she put on a magical belt loaned to her by Aphrodite, the goddess of **erotic** or sexual love. The magic waistband made Hera irresistible to Zeus. Overwhelmed with **amorous** feelings, he made love to his wife and shortly afterward fell asleep. Hera then snuck away to help the Trojans.

10. enamored (ih NAM urd) adj. in a condition in which you love, admire, or are extremely interested in someone or something
Synonyms: infatuated, fascinated, charmed, captivated, **enthralled** (in THRAWLD)

Confusion reigns in Shakespeare's magical, light-hearted comedy *A Midsummer Night's Dream*. A special flower creates hilarious situations by making those in love with their partners instantly despise them and become **enamored** with those they might have previously scorned. The juice of this magical flower, when dropped upon a sleeping person's eyelids, causes that person to be **enamored** with the first thing they see upon waking. Oberon, the king of the fairies, has quarreled with Titania, his queen, and wants to punish her. He therefore anoints her eyelids with the flower's juice. Upon waking, she sees a man whose head has been transformed into that of an ass or donkey. Upon seeing this man with his ridiculous ears and elongated snout, she immediately becomes **enthralled** with this monstrosity. Oberon eventually feels better toward Titania and removes the spell. She tells Oberon, "What visions I have seen! / Methought I was **enamored** of an ass." Of course, the word "**enamored**" does not have to apply to only amorous situations. One can be **enamored** or **enthralled** with a painting, a piece of music, Shakespeare's plays, Greek mythology, or even with the sound, meaning, and etymology of words themselves.

WORKING WITH WORDS

UNIT 5, LESSON 9

I. Complete the sentences by using each of the following words once:

durable, amorous, avert, endure, revert
obdurate, divert, duress, enamored, subvert

1. Once you have shed the desired pounds and fat on a healthy, well-balanced diet, you must maintain proper eating habits or you will __________ to your former condition.

2. Diana became so __________ with her introductory college chemistry course that she decided to major in chemistry and today makes breakthrough discoveries for a pharmaceutical company.

3. The Greek mythological Oedipus tried to __________ the fulfillment of a prophecy that said he would kill his father and marry his mother; he fled from the couple who adopted him as an infant only to arrive at a kingdom where unknowingly he killed his biological father and married the woman who gave him birth.

4. My doctor said either I have an operation on my spine or __________ back pain for the rest of my life.

5. The FBI uncovered a plot by foreign agents who tried to __________ our public health programs by making our vaccines ineffective.

6. Although the captured soldier endured torture, he refused to sign a false statement under __________.

7. Attracted to the handsome man who made __________ advances to her, the devoted wife nevertheless resisted his seduction.

8. He was so focused on studying for his final examinations that nothing could __________ his attention.

9. My __________ old coat has kept me warm for the last forty winters.

10. The __________ owner of the company stubbornly kept to his habitual methods and refused to listen to his children's advice on how to modernize and increase production.

II. This exercise reinforces the difficult synonyms in boldface accompanying the main words derived from word parts. Select the two words that are synonyms.

1.	a. stubborn	b. mean
	c. necessary	d. obstinate
2.	a. persevere	b. continue
	c. make love	d. reduce
3.	a. enthralled	b. upset
	c. patient	d. fascinated
4.	a. resist	b. force
	c. undermine	d. ruin
5.	a. sexual	b. powerful
	c. erotic	d. excessive
6.	a. regress	b. go back
	c. rub	d. annoy
7.	a. abiding	b. lasting
	c. temporary	d. humorous
8.	a. distract	b. loosen
	c. sidetrack	d. lose
9.	a. confidence	b. guilt
	c. coercion	d. pressure
10.	a. increase	b. capture
	c. forestall	d. prevent

UNIT 5
LESSON 10

Prefixes in the following words are underlined.
See page xiv for list of prefixes and their definitions.

Word Parts and Words
AM (love): amiable, amity
VIV (live): <u>con</u>vivial, vivacious, <u>re</u>vive, vivid
TRI (T) (rub, wear away): trite, <u>con</u>trite, <u>at</u>trition, <u>de</u>trimental

AM — love (amateur)

11. amiable (AY mee uh bul) adj. friendly, agreeable, good-natured
Related Forms: amiability, amiableness, amiably
Synonyms: likeable, easygoing, pleasant, **affable** (AF uh bul)
Antonyms: unfriendly, disagreeable, unpleasant, surly

Hell and damnation are not usually associated with **amiableness** and **affability**. We often think of sin as horrid, repulsive, and revolting, but if it were not attractive, who would be tempted by it? Mephistopheles, the tempting devil from hell, appears prominently in two plays based on the Faust legend. In this legend, an elderly scholar makes a compact with the devil exchanging his soul for certain powers. The Englishman Christopher Marlowe, a contemporary of Shakespeare's, gives his version of the legend and the devil in the play *Dr. Faustus* (1588). About two hundred years later, the German Johann Wolfgang von Goethe wrote *Faust*. In this play Faust is an elderly scholar who compacts with the devil to become once again a young man. Goethe's Mephistopheles appears not so much as an antagonist opponent but as an **amiable**, sophisticated companion to Faust. Mephistopheles presents himself as an **affable** comrade with his witty, amusing, cynical sense of humor. Both Marlowe and

Goethe's plays deserve to be read. Personally, I prefer *Faust*, not only because of the seemingly **amiable** and **affable** tempting agent from hell, but because of the profound questions the play raises.

12. amity (AM uh tee) n. friendly or peaceful relationship
Synonyms: friendship, harmony, goodwill, **accord** (uh KAWRD)
Antonyms: enmity, animosity, ill-will, discord

The twentieth century saw the establishment of two organizations to promote **amity** among the world's nations: the League of Nations and the United Nations (UN). Following World War I, the League was set up in 1920 to maintain **accord** and thus avoid another catastrophic war. Ironically, even though U.S. President Woodrow Wilson pioneered the idea of the League, the United States never became a member. The League failed to avert another world war as the powerful nations of Germany and Japan also never joined. The United Nations was formed in 1945 after World War II ended. Unlike the League, the UN has all the world's major powers as members. Hopefully, the UN will help reduce hostility by furthering international **amity** and **accord**.

VIV — live (survive, survival)

13. convivial (kun VIV ee ul) adj. sociable, cheerful, festive
Related Forms: conviviality, convivially
Synonyms: social, friendly, gregarious, **genial** (JEEN yul)
Antonyms: unsociable, reserved, staid, reticent, taciturn, stolid

U.S presidents have varied greatly in personality. Theodore Roosevelt, who served as chief executive from 1901-1909, had a **convivial** nature that exuded charisma. **Genial** and full of energy, he happily joined friends in tennis, hiking, horseback riding, and even swimming in the icy Potomac. Calvin Coolidge was much more reserved. Coolidge, who as vice-president became president when Warren Harding died in office in 1923, held the presidency until 1929. Exuberant **conviviality** and lively **geniality** were not his trademark. A man known not to indulge in unnecessary speech, he was nicknamed "Silent Cal." Once at a social affair a woman told Coolidge that she had bet she could get him to speak more than two words. Coolidge replied, "You lose."

14. vivacious (vih VAY shus) adj. full of spirit and enthusiasm, lively
Related Forms: vivacity, vivaciousness, vivaciously
Synonyms: spirited, sparkling, animated, effervescent, scintillating, **ebullient** (ih BOOL yunt)
Antonyms: dull, boring, lifeless, listless, languid

Vivacious and **ebullient** perfectly describe the heroine Rosalind in Shakespeare's comedy *As You Like It.* Spirited, witty, wise, Rosalind has an irrepressible capacity for joy. The evil Duke Frederick banishes Rosalind from court and she flees to the forest, but not before she and Orlando meet and instantly fall mutually in love. Shortly afterward, Orlando, too, must escape to the forest. Nothing can squelch Rosalind's spirit. She assumes the disguise of a boy and maintains a positive outlook. There she meets Orlando, who does not recognize her. He pours out his feelings of love toward Rosalind, unaware that he is actually speaking to her. Rosalind playfully tells him that she will act the part of his beloved and cure him of his love sickness. She enjoys teasing Orlando about love and can speak mockingly of it, all the while fully aware of her own passion for Orlando. Her liveliness, incisive jesting remarks, and capacity for playfulness make the **vivacious** Rosalind one of Shakespeare's most appealing characters. The play concludes with the ever **ebullient** Rosalind revealing her true identity and marrying Orlando.

15. revive (rih VYV) v. return or restore to life, consciousness, health; bring back into use
Related Forms: revivify, revival, revivification, reviver, revivable
Synonyms: restore, **resuscitate** (rih SUs uh TAYT)

16. vivid (VIV id) adj. clear, intense, bright (as in color, language, or an image); brilliant; distinct
Related Forms: vividness, vividly
Synonyms: colorful, radiant, **vibrant** (VY brunt)
Antonyms: vague, unclear, hazy, dull, colorless

The Dutch painter Vincent Van Gogh (1853-1890) sold only one painting in his life. Although he had little recognition in his lifetime, Van Gogh's reputation dramatically **revived** in the twentieth century. Too bad Van Gogh himself could not be **resuscitated** to enjoy his success. **Vivid** color often characterizes his landscapes, still lifes, and portraits. Now these **vibrant** paintings sell for millions of dollars.

TRI(T) [Do not confuse this word part with TRI meaning "three"] — rub, wear away (detriment, contrition)

17. trite (TRYT) adj. uninteresting because of overuse; lacking originality and freshness
Related Forms: triteness, tritely
Synonyms: well-worn, overused, stale, commonplace, banal, **hackneyed** (HAK need)
Antonyms: fresh, original, imaginative

18. contrite (kun TRYT) adj. expressing grief, sorrow, regret for one's sins or faults
Related Forms: contrition, contritely
Synonyms: sorry, regretful, apologetic, remorseful, **penitent** (PEN uh tunt)
Antonyms: unrepentant, impenitent

19. attrition (uh TRISH un) n. gradual reduction in number or strength; rubbing away or wearing down bit by bit
Synonyms: weakening, reduction, deterioration, attenuation, **erosion** (ih ROH zhun)
Antonyms: reinforcement, build up, accretion, strengthening

20. detrimental (deh trih MEN tul) adj. harmful, damaging
Related Forms: detriment, detrimentally
Synonyms: injurious, hurtful, **deleterious** (del ih TEER ee us)
Antonyms: beneficial, benign, favorable

The etymology or origin of words helps us to associate groups of words and learn their meanings. Rubbing off the modern surface of meaning of the above four words, we can track them back to their Latin source *tritus* ("rub away," "worn out"). A **trite** expression is one that is overused and has thus worn out the shining brilliance of its early coinage. "**Hackneyed,**" a synonym of "**trite**," traces its origin back to the English town of Hackney, known for its horses which were overworked as they drew carriages which came to be called "hackneys." Etymologies help us understand why worn out, uninteresting, and dull remarks are described as **trite** and **hackneyed**. Ebenezer Scrooge in Charles Dickens's *A Christmas Carol* becomes **penitent** after being visited by the Ghosts of Christmas Past, Christmas Present, and Christmas Future. **Contrite** individuals have been worn down by regret for past actions and want their burden of guilt lifted. A war of **attrition** is not won in a single quick strike. Rather, the war goes on and on until one side is gradually worn down, just as water slowly causes **erosion** of rock and after millions of years produces such wonders as the Grand Canyon. Alcohol abuse and cigarette smoking, lack of exercise, and poor diet all wear away our health and result in **deleterious** effects. Avoid practices that are **detrimental** to physical, mental, and spiritual well-being.

WORKING WITH WORDS

UNIT 5, LESSONS 9 & 10

The following exercises include all main words derived from word parts and their synonyms in boldface from both Lessons 9 and 10.

I. Match the word on the left with its synonym.

Set 1

____1. convivial	a. erotic, passionate
____2. subvert	b. hackneyed, commonplace
____3. trite	c. vibrant, clear
____4. amity	d. sidetrack, distract
____5. duress	e. persevere, last
____6. vivid	f. genial, sociable
____7. divert	g. undermine, overthrow
____8. endure	h. erosion, reduction
____9. amorous	i. coercion, intimidation
____10. attrition	j. accord, friendship

Set 2

____1. durable	a. resuscitate, restore
____2. vivacious	b. deleterious, injurious
____3. revive	c. obstinate, stubborn
____4. avert	d. affable, friendly
____5. enamored	e. ebullient, lively
____6. obdurate	f. enthralled, fascinated
____7. contrite	g. regress, return
____8. detrimental	h. forestall, avoid
____9. amiable	i. penitent, sorry
____10. revert	j. abiding, long-lasting

II. Complete the following sentences by using each of the following words only once:

Set 1 Words:
durable, amity, vivid, detrimental, duress, trite, divert, convivial, amorous, avert

1. My teacher says that my phrasing and ideas are ____________; I must try to be more original and imaginative.

2. Perhaps we discover more stone tools from the ancient past than those made of wood because stone is more ____________ than wood.

3. We want ____________ people at our party, not those who are withdrawn and avoid participation in any activity.

4. Jennifer rejected the ____________ attention of James since she had no romantic interest in him.

5. You can shoot me if you want, but I will never sign that document under ____________ .

6. Excessive absences and handing in assignments late will be ____________ to your grade.

7. We must strive for ____________ among nations; the vengeful attitude of "an eye for an eye" only promotes hostility, and as Gandhi (India's father of independence) said, will leave the whole world blind.

8. Nothing can ____________ the focused attention of Margaret when she studies for final examinations.

9. The memory of when I almost drowned is so ____________ that I can recall every detail of the event even though it happened over forty years ago.

10. In the ancient Greek tragedy *Oedipus the King* by Sophocles, the oracle tells Oedipus that he will kill his father and marry his mother. Oedipus tries to ____________ this tragedy by running away from whom he believes are his father and mother. Actually,

this couple adopted Oedipus but never told him. Fleeing his home, Oedipus unknowingly reaches the kingdom of his biological parents. Through a series of events, he fulfills the horrible prophecy and thus shows that fate cannot be averted.

Set 2 Words:
subvert, obdurate, enamored, revert, endure, revived, amiable, attrition, contrite, vivacious

1. People living near the North Pole ______________ long, harsh winters.

2. The startled dog turned around and bit the woman; when the dog saw that the woman was its owner, it felt sorry and ______________ as it tried to lick its master's wound.

3. "As stubborn as a mule" has become a trite saying that means as ______________ as a mule.

4. After being in a coma for two months, my uncle ______________ and fully recovered.

5. The teacher thought that unruly students were trying to ______________ his efforts to educate them.

6. Romeo and Juliet were instantly ______________ with each other.

7. Warning: If after enduring a restrained and healthy diet for several months that enabled you to shed pounds of excess fat, you ______________ to your unhealthy diet of junk food, you will rapidly regain weight.

8. My parents told me to avoid being disagreeable and to be friendly or ______________ to our rich uncle if we expected to be helped with paying our college tuition.

9. Our workforce diminishes through ______________ since those who retire are not replaced with new employees.

10. My lively, enthusiastic, ______________ aunt filled me with joy whenever she appeared.

III. LOVE: SHAKESPEARE AND ST. PAUL

Fill in each blank by using each of the following words only once:

Set 1 Words:

amity, amorous, enamored, duress, obdurate, vivacious, conviviality, avert, amiable, contrite

We love our girlfriends, boyfriends, wives and husbands. We love our children. We love our parents. We love movies. We love sports. We love science. We love our jobs. We love money. We love to read. We love to eat. We love to relax. We love when someone stops telling us what to do. What is love? We associate the word with so many various experiences. Here will consider two kinds of love: romantic and sexual love as depicted in Shakespeare's tragic play *Romeo and Juliet*, and love as described by St. Paul in his first letter to the Corinthians in the Bible.

In the opening scene of Shakespeare's play we find the __________ or passionate Romeo moping because Rosalind, the girl he is enamored with, has rejected him. He then learns of a party hosted by the Capulets where Rosalind will be present. Romeo's friend, hoping to divert or distract Romeo from his gloomy state, says he will accompany Romeo to the party where the rejected lover will see many girls far more attractive than Rosalind.

Capulet, the head of the family hosting the affair, recognizes Romeo. Although the Capulets are not on __________ or friendly terms with Romeo's family of the Montagues—the two families have been bitterly feuding with each other for generations—Capulet does not want the __________ or cheerful festivity destroyed and allows Romeo to participate. Romeo then sees Capulet's daughter, Juliet. They dance with each other while flirtatiously exchanging lines that end with a kiss. Romeo does not know she is Capulet's daughter, and she is unaware that he is a Montague. Romeo finds her far more beautiful and __________ or lively than Rosalind. In fact, they instantly become completely __________ or infatuated with each other. It is love at first sight.

Romeo and Juliet then secretly get married by Friar Laurence. However, Capulet has arranged a marriage for Juliet to someone else. He tells of this coming marriage and finds her most ____________ or stubborn in her refusal. Her rejection of his proposal enrages Capulet (a father had almost complete control of his family in this time period and a daughter was usually expected to conform to his wishes) and he even threatens to disown Juliet if she will not marry the man of his choice. Under ____________ or threat of her father's punishment, Juliet seeks advice from Friar Laurence. He tells her to agree to her father's command. The Friar has a plan to ____________ or prevent the marriage. He gives her a potion to take the night before the wedding. The potion will cause her to appear dead for a period of forty-two hours. The Capulets will then put her in an open tomb. Friar Laurence will then get word to Romeo (who meanwhile has been banished from the city for killing a member of the Capulet family in a duel) of what happened and to return to Juliet before she wakes. The couple will then leave their native city and return when the Friar deems it appropriate.

Unfortunately, the Friar's message never gets to Romeo. He hears of her death, returns to the tomb before she wakes, and believing her dead, kills himself by drinking poison. She awakes, sees Romeo dead, takes his dagger and plunges it into her heart. The Capulets and Montagues arrive at the tomb and witness the deaths that their enmity or hostility and hatred for each other have caused. They are now ____________ or regretful for their feud and agree to set up golden statues to commemorate the lovers. ____________ or a peaceful relationship is restored between the Montagues and Capulets but at the tragic price of the deaths of Romeo and Juliet.

Set 2 Words:
attrition, reverted, durable, trite, subvert, revived, vivid, divert, endured, detrimental

Romeo and Juliet appeals because of its superb rendering of love that combines erotic passion with the innocence of youth. Although we do not doubt the purity and intensity of their mutual attraction to each other, we expect that if Romeo and Juliet would have lived a long life together which involved the daily affairs of maintaining a household and raising children, the nature of their love for each other would have changed. The laser-like intensity and focus of their infatuation would transform into a more realistic and comprehensive assessment of each other. By contrast, St. Paul depicts a love not centered on obtaining the desired romantic object of one's life, but a love that is entirely selfless and self-giving.

A contemporary of Jesus, Paul never met Jesus while Jesus was alive. Like Jesus, Paul was Jewish, but Paul was not initially a follower of Jesus. In fact, Paul persecuted Jews who accepted Jesus as their Savior. On the way to Damascus, Syria, to arrest Jews who were now Christians, Paul experienced a flash of light from heaven and heard the voice of Jesus. For three days after this incident he remained blind. When his sight was restored his soul was ____________ or restored as well. This vision of Jesus (occurring after Jesus's physical death) transformed Paul forever. From persecutor of Christians he became the foremost missionary of Christianity, especially to non-Jews. Paul never ____________ or returned to his former condition of persecuting Jewish followers of Jesus. Traveling to Cyprus, Asia Minor, and Greece to introduce Christianity, Paul ____________ or suffered such ____________ or harmful occurrences as flogging, stoning, and death threats. Such attacks on Paul amounted to a virtual war of ____________ to ____________ or undermine his work. However, the ____________ or long-lasting and sturdy Paul kept to his purpose. Nothing could ____________ or turn Paul aside from his mission until he eventually suffered a martyr's death.

In essence, Paul was spreading Jesus's message of love. Paul described this love in no ___trite___ or commonplace terms. In his first letter to the Corinthians, found in the New Testament of the Bible, Paul defined this selfless and self-giving love with ___vivid___ or clear, distinct, and striking language:

> Love is patient; love is kind; love is not envious or boastful or arrogant or rude. It does not insist on its own way; it is not irritable or resentful; it does not rejoice in wrongdoing, but rejoices in truth. It bears all things, believes all things, hopes all things, endures all things.

MASTER EXERCISES

Select the definition closest in meaning in the following exercises.

I. This exercise reviews all major entry words.

1. adhere
   (a) repel (b) stick
   (c) loosen (d) divide

2. affable
   (a) funny (b) grumpy
   (c) friendly (d) talkative

3. allude
   (a) suggest (b) invent
   (c) cry (d) focus

4. amiable
   (a) friendly (b) curious
   (c) angry (d) anxious

5. amity
   (a) opposition (b) friendship
   (c) excitement (d) illusion

6. amorous
   (a) suffocating (b) delicious
   (c) precious (d) passionate

7. anarchy
   (a) order (b) dictatorship
   (c) democracy (d) lawlessness

8. apprehensive
   (a) worried (b) unconcerned
   (c) respectful (d) unknown

9. apprehend
   (a) let go (b) arrest
   (c) start (d) finish

10. assimilate	(a) confuse	(b) lose
	(c) charm	(d) absorb
11. attrition	(a) wearing down	(b) murder
	(c) benefit	(d) decision
12. auspicious	(a) unlucky	(b) destructive
	(c) favorable	(d) decisive
13. avert	(a) proceed	(b) unlock
	(c) twist	(d) prevent
14. bona fide	(a) sinister	(b) helpful
	(c) genuine	(d) pitiful
15. circumlocution	(a) circumstance	(b) forgery
	(c) imagination	(d) roundabout speech
16. circumspect	(a) unusual	(b) usual
	(c) cautious	(d) false
17. coherent	(a) weak	(b) logically consistent
	(c) unforgettable	(d) excessively talkative
18. collusion	(a) hatred	(b) conspiracy
	(c) celebration	(d) collision
19. compensate	(a) make up for	(b) take from
	(c) enter to	(d) exit from
20. comprehensive	(a) unknown	(b) attractive
	(c) vicious	(d) complete
21. conspicuous	(a) obvious	(b) vague
	(c) religious	(d) questioning

22. contrite
(a) honest (b) joyous
(c) sorry (d) thankful

23. convivial
(a) late (b) on time
(c) early (d) sociable

24. degrade
(a) promote (b) lower
(c) believe (d) doubt

25. desultory
(a) unoccupied (b) determined
(c) aimless (d) impatient

26. detrimental
(a) wicked (b) relaxed
(c) harmful (d) productive

27. dichotomy
(a) division (b) defeat
(c) scorn (d) anger

28. diffident
(a) uncertain (b) burdensome
(c) beautiful (d) shy

29. digress
(a) stray (b) maintain
(c) return (d) surrender

30. distort
(a) misshape (b) magnify
(c) mislead (d) minimalize

31. divert
(a) reproduce (b) complain
(c) sympathize with (d) turn aside

32. durable
(a) lasting (b) vanishing
(c) shiny (d) dull

33. duress
(a) kindness (b) assistance
(c) threat (d) cooperation

34. egress
(a) entrance (b) view
(c) choice (d) exit

35. eloquent
(a) loud (b) clumsy
(c) rough (d) fluent

36. elusive
(a) slippery (b) similar
(c) nonsensical (d) sticky

37. enamored
(a) rejected (b) broken
(c) in debt (d) in love

38. endure
(a) disintegrate (b) last
(c) reproduce (d) disappear

39. entomology
(a) stamp collecting (b) coin collecting
(c) plant study (d) insect study

40. epitome
(a) example (b) seed
(c) scientist (d) occupant

41. equanimity
(a) rage (b) calm
(c) power (d) weakness

42. equity
(a) preacher (b) witness
(c) fairness (d) danger

43. equivocal
(a) truthful (b) ambiguous
(c) educated (d) proven

44. eulogy
(a) tribute (b) punishment
(c) curse (d) contract

45. euphemism
(a) curse word (b) polite term
(c) correction (d) solution

46. euphoria	(a) wisdom	(b) bliss
	(c) memory loss	(d) suffering
47. euthanasia	(a) mercy killing	(b) falling in love
	(c) preparation	(d) preservation
48. extort	(a) get by threat	(b) tempt
	(c) debate	(d) deny
49. facsimile	(a) invention	(b) mistake
	(c) perfection	(d) copy
50. fidelity	(a) treachery	(b) loyalty
	(c) courage	(d) hospitality
51. hierarchy	(a) observation	(b) conclusion
	(c) ranking	(d) promise
52. impending	(a) spending	(b) preventing
	(c) saving	(d) coming
53. importune	(a) beg	(b) refuse
	(c) exercise	(d) get rich
54. impotent	(a) powerful	(b) powerless
	(c) unsatisfactory	(d) satisfactory
55. incoherent	(a) incomprehensible	(b) logical
	(c) unified	(d) furious
56. ineffable	(a) unloved	(b) unfamiliar
	(c) effective	(d) indescribable
57. inequity	(a) teamwork	(b) seriousness
	(c) unfairness	(d) revenge

58. infamy	(a) childhood	(b) regret
	(c) disgrace	(d) reaction
59. inherent	(a) spoiled	(b) inborn
	(c) learned	(d) forgotten
60. impugn	(a) attack	(b) fall asleep
	(c) accept	(d) arouse
61. loquacious	(a) boring	(b) funny
	(c) disgusting	(d) talkative
62. ludicrous	(a) ridiculous	(b) concerned
	(c) exhausted	(d) profitable
63. matriarch	(a) male ruler	(b) female ruler
	(c) child ruler	(d) lawlessness
64. monarch	(a) loser	(b) enemy
	(c) sovereign	(d) messenger
65. monolithic	(a) scattered	(b) uniform
	(c) accurate	(d) uninformed
66. monologue	(a) one person talking	(b) debate
	(c) confusion	(d) peace
67. monotheism	(a) absence of belief	(b) belief in one God
	(c) worship of trees	(d) belief in many gods
68. monotonous	(a) exciting	(b) sensible
	(c) loud	(d) boring
69. nefarious	(a) slow	(b) clever
	(c) luxurious	(d) wicked

70. obdurate (a) permissible (b) convincing
(c) generous (d) stubborn

71. obloquy (a) habit (b) reward
(c) condemnation (d) disease

72. omnipotent (a) reluctant (b) unprepared
(c) all-powerful (d) all-knowing

73. pensive (a) pleasant (b) thoughtful
(c) reckless (d) secure

74. perfidy (a) recognition (b) treachery
(c) blindness (d) speechless

75. portend (a) acquire (b) give away
(c) foreshadow (d) condemn

76. portly (a) wise (b) handsome
(c) fat (d) old

77. potent (a) narrow (b) rich
(c) cruel (d) powerful

78. potentate (a) slave (b) cook
(c) ruler (d) guest

79. propensity (a) hatred (b) opinion
(c) tendency (d) exploration

80. pugilist (a) victim (b) boxer
(c) leader (d) follower

81. pugnacious (a) spiritual (b) combative
(c) alert (d) easily led

82. rapport	(a) contest	(b) conference
	(c) funeral service	(d) good relationship
83. reprehensible	(a) blameworthy	(b) praiseworthy
	(c) brilliant	(d) dull
84. repugnant	(a) disgusting	(b) tempting
	(c) jealous	(d) unmistakable
85. resilient	(a) firm	(b) foolish
	(c) giving up	(d) quickly adjusting
86. retort	(a) get together	(b) reply
	(c) exit	(d) enter
87. revert	(a) capture	(b) help
	(c) return	(d) vanish
88. revive	(a) listen	(b) respect
	(c) restore	(d) inform
89. salient	(a) busy	(b) lazy
	(c) unfortunate	(d) outstanding
90. sally	(a) attack	(b) cure
	(c) defend	(d) intercept
91. simile	(a) detour	(b) question
	(c) comparison	(d) guest
92. simulate	(a) repel	(b) bargain
	(c) argue	(d) imitate
93. specious	(a) misleading	(b) advising
	(c) respectful	(d) obnoxious

94. subvert — (a) overthrow (b) establish (c) deny (d) inform

95. tome — (a) statue (b) painting (c) weapon (d) book

96. tortuous — (a) twisting (b) painful (c) threatening (d) emotional

97. transgression — (a) knowledge (b) violation (c) travel (d) election

98. trite — (a) overused (b) refreshing (c) effective (d) hurtful

99. vivacious — (a) lively (b) deceptive (c) weak (d) valuable

100. vivid — (a) thoughtful (b) easygoing (c) brilliant (d) complete

II. Review of all the synonyms that were reinforced by exercises in the individual lessons.

1. abhorrent	(a) remarkable (c) pleasant	(b) disgusting (d) impatient
2. abiding	(a) distinguished (c) foreign	(b) restless (d) lasting
3. accord	(a) injury (c) surprise	(b) anger (d) harmony
4. affable	(a) friendly (c) thankful	(b) victorious (d) vicious
5. ambiguous	(a) unhappy (c) brave	(b) happy (d) unclear
6. amiable	(a) friendly (c) swift	(b) undecided (d) confused
7. analogy	(a) resistance (c) comparison	(b) permission (d) ceremony
8. articulate	(a) happy (c) fluent	(b) rough (d) trustworthy
9. assail	(a) navigate (c) repeat	(b) prepare (d) attack
10. authentic	(a) fake (c) intelligent	(b) expensive (d) genuine
11. belligerent	(a) active (c) peaceful	(b) required (d) combative

12. bias (a) prejudice (b) relaxation
(c) heavy burden (d) justice

13. buoyant (a) new (b) required
(c) horrible (d) cheerfully adjusting

14. camaraderie (a) revenge (b) fellowship
(c) creativity (d) boredom

15. culpable (a) honest (b) poor
(c) wealthy (d) blameworthy

16. circuitous (a) reluctant (b) roundabout
(c) insane (d) bold

17. circumlocution (a) nonsense (b) roundabout speech
(c) competition (d) wealth

18. coerce (a) force (b) promote
(c) stop (d) solve

19. coercion (a) force (b) promotion
(c) stop (d) solution

20. cogent (a) unclear (b) logical
(c) complete (d) empty

21. cohere (a) stick (b) refuse
(c) punish (d) reward

22. composure (a) calm (b) surroundings
(c) anxiety (d) voyage

23. conspicuous (a) excited (b) dull
(c) accurate (d) noticeable

24. conspiracy
(a) vacation (b) promotion
(c) observation (d) collusion

25. contemplative
(a) famous (b) unified
(c) thoughtful (d) repulsive

26. debase
(a) praise (b) lower
(c) win (d) starve

27. deity
(a) villain (b) god
(c) winner (d) loser

28. deleterious
(a) helpful (b) permissive
(c) early (d) harmful

29. deviate
(a) stray (b) remain
(c) insist (d) devour

30. discernible
(a) imitative (b) successful
(c) unfortunate (d) noticeable

31. duplicity
(a) origin (b) destination
(c) gift (d) deceit

32. ebullient
(a) uncertain (b) certain
(c) cheerful (d) cruel

33. efficacious
(a) important (b) beautiful
(c) effective (d) empty

34. elation
(a) despair (b) joy
(c) honor (d) poverty

35. embodiment
(a) bodily example (b) tomb
(c) originality (d) acceptance speech

36. enthralled	(a) satisfactory	(b) punished
	(c) captivated	(d) disgusted
37. entreat	(a) plead	(b) denounce
	(c) donate	(d) prosper
38. erosion	(a) building up	(b) wearing away
	(c) tropical forest	(d) conservation
39. erotic	(a) sexual	(b) gift
	(c) promise	(d) monument
40. etymology	(a) bird study	(b) fish study
	(c) word origin	(d) insect study
41. evasive	(a) slippery	(b) truthful
	(c) beneficial	(d) sickly
42. exodus	(a) departure	(b) entrance
	(c) nutrition	(d) progress
43. extensive	(a) preventing	(b) minimal
	(c) wide-ranging	(d) destructive
44. fallacious	(a) mature	(b) false
	(c) destructive	(d) accidental
45. feign	(a) jump	(b) fight
	(c) embrace	(d) fake
46. forestall	(a) predict	(b) supply
	(c) prevent	(d) promote
47. garrulous	(a) talkative	(b) precious
	(c) silent	(d) worthless

48. genial
(a) friendly (b) bitter
(c) humorous (d) wise

49. hackneyed
(a) stationary (b) original
(c) overused (d) strict

50. haphazard
(a) organized (b) lazy
(c) unsystematic (d) dangerous

51. homogenize
(a) blend (b) drink
(c) imagine (d) plan

52. homogenous
(a) isolated (b) uniform
(c) suffocating (d) imaginative

53. imminent
(a) near (b) warm
(c) populated (d) empty

54. impartiality
(a) distribution (b) government
(c) fairness (d) revolution

55. imply
(a) demand (b) offer
(c) suggest (d) capture

56. inarticulate
(a) clear (b) incomprehensible
(c) wordy (d) brief

57. incarcerate
(a) imprison (b) threaten
(c) reorganize (d) put to sleep

58. incursion
(a) warning (b) invitation
(c) attack (d) prophecy

59. ineffectual
(a) skillful (b) lifeless
(c) ineffective (d) dominant

60. infringement	(a) violation	(b) communication
	(c) foundation	(d) insight
61. iniquitous	(a) healthy	(b) wicked
	(c) weak	(d) marvelous
62. intrinsic	(a) absent	(b) powerful
	(c) essential	(d) evil
63. martial artist	(a) sculptor	(b) architect
	(c) fighter	(d) law officer
64. matron	(a) woman leader	(b) comedian
	(c) tragic actor	(d) politician
65. misconstrue	(a) overlook	(b) misinterpret
	(c) steal	(d) donate
66. nihilism	(a) anarchy	(b) order
	(c) destruction	(d) forgetfulness
67. notoriety	(a) passion	(b) bad reputation
	(c) false identity	(d) forecast
68. obese	(a) handsome	(b) talented
	(c) dangerous	(d) fat
69. obstinate	(a) proud	(b) humble
	(c) stubborn	(d) dynamic
70. opus	(a) copy	(b) major work
	(c) office	(d) musician
71. palliative	(a) educational	(b) soothing
	(c) injurious	(d) descriptive

72. panegyric
(a) praise (b) guilt
(c) discovery (d) division

73. pecking order
(a) battle (b) ranking
(c) success (d) military

74. penitent
(a) annoying (b) extreme
(c) sorry (d) happy

75. persevere
(a) fail (b) continue
(c) damage (d) abuse

76. perturbed
(a) worried (b) drowsy
(c) committed (d) injured

77. potentate
(a) ruler (b) enemy
(c) healer (d) athlete

78. predilection
(a) union (b) preference
(c) separation (d) compromise

79. preeminent
(a) small (b) weak
(c) supreme (d) bashful

80. preposterous
(a) smart (b) painful
(c) outstanding (d) absurd

81. presage
(a) annoy (b) purify
(c) foretell (d) mourn

82. propitious
(a) nasty (b) vigorous
(c) favorable (d) unique

83. prudent
(a) daring (b) cautious
(c) respectable (d) secret

84. regress	(a) renew	(b) reunite
	(c) return	(d) review
85. reimburse	(a) repay	(b) remember
	(c) reply	(d) regard
86. replica	(a) copy	(b) punishment
	(c) renewal	(d) objection
87. resuscitate	(a) immigrate	(b) renounce
	(c) insist	(d) restore
88. riposte	(a) shield	(b) tunnel
	(c) reply	(d) lecture
89. schism	(a) congratulations	(b) congregation
	(c) rejection	(d) split
90. sidetrack	(a) concentrate	(b) daydream
	(c) turn aside	(d) follow
91. sinuous	(a) winding	(b) straight
	(c) efficient	(d) corrupt
92. soliloquy	(a) dialogue	(b) audience
	(c) monologue	(d) entrance
93. sovereign	(a) passenger	(b) drama
	(c) newcomer	(d) ruler
94. steadfastness	(a) hope	(b) jealousy
	(c) protest	(d) devotion
95. tedious	(a) adventurous	(b) boring
	(c) generous	(d) aggressive

96. timorous
(a) inventive
(b) nervously insecure
(c) loud
(d) extremely rude

97. undermine
(a) activate
(b) resent
(c) weaken
(d) support

98. unutterable
(a) unspeakable
(b) growling
(c) descriptive
(d) complaining

99. vibrant
(a) deadly
(b) shaky
(c) upset
(d) brilliant

100. vilification
(a) defamation
(b) worship
(c) announcement
(d) cooperation

Index

The word parts are CAPITALIZED. The 100 main entry words derived from the word parts are in **boldface**, and words with exercises are in *italics*.